D0439485

SECOND CORINTHIANS

SECOND CORINTHIANS

By

G. COLEMAN LUCK

MOODY PRESS • CHICAGO

ISBN: 0-8024-2047-8

Printed in the United States of America

CONTENTS

Chapter One

INTRODUCTORY THOUGHTS

I<small>N</small> E<small>PHESUS</small>, the chief city of the Roman province of Asia, the apostle Paul ministered for no less than three years during his third great missionary journey. At this city Paul wrote his First Epistle to the church at Corinth. The hand of the Lord was manifestly upon his work at Ephesus, and many were saved. There was also great danger to be faced. Paul refers to this in II Corinthians 1:8: "For we would not, brethren, have you ignorant of our trouble which came to us in Asia, that we were pressed out of measure, above strength, insomuch that we despaired even of life."

From Ephesus Paul went on to Troas, where he expected to meet Titus, whom he had sent to Corinth. The fact that he did not find his beloved fellow laborer there gave him great concern. "Furthermore, when I came to Troas to preach Christ's gospel, and a door was opened unto me of the Lord, I had no rest in my spirit, because I found not Titus my brother: but taking my leave of them, I went from thence into Macedonia" (II Cor. 2:12, 13). In Macedonia Titus finally met Paul. He brought to the apostle a generally favorable report as to the conduct of the Corinthians Christians after they had received his previous letter. "For, when we were come into Macedonia, our flesh had no rest, but we were troubled on every side; without were fightings, within were fears. Nevertheless God, that comforteth those that are cast down, comforted us by the coming of Titus; And not by his coming only, but by the consolation wherewith he was comforted in you, when he told us your earnest desire, your mourning, your fervent mind toward me; so that I rejoiced the more. For though I made you sorry with a letter, I do not repent, though I did repent: for I perceive that the same epistle hath made you sorry, though it were but for a season. Now I rejoice, not that ye were made sorry, but that ye sorrowed to repentance: for ye were made sorry after a godly manner, that ye might receive damage by us in nothing. For godly sorrow worketh repentance to salvation not to be repented of: but the sorrow of the world worketh death. For behold this selfsame thing, that ye sorrowed after a godly sort, what carefulness it wrought in you, yea, what clearing of yourselves, yea, what indignation, yea, what fear, yea, what vehement desire, yea, what zeal, yea, what revenge! In all things ye have approved yourselves to be clear in this matter" (II Cor. 7:5-11).

First Corinthians had been written to correct certain problems which existed in the church. The report from Titus indicated that these had been almost cleared up. However Paul found that a second letter was needed for several reasons:

1. He was now afraid that the Corinthians might be too severe with the chief offender in their church. Paul had previously urged strong discipline for this man (I Cor. 5): Now he writes: "But if any have caused grief, he hath not grieved me, but in part: that I may not overcharge you all. Sufficient to such a man is this punishment, which was inflicted of many.

So that contrariwise ye ought rather to forgive him, and comfort him, lest perhaps such a one should be swallowed up with overmuch sorrow. Wherefore I beseech you that ye would confirm your love toward him. For to this end also did I write, that I might know the proof of you, whether ye be obedient in all things. To whom ye forgive anything, I forgive also: for if I forgave anything, to whom I forgave it, for your sakes forgave I it in the person of Christ; Lest Satan should get an advantage of us: for we are not ignorant of his devices" (II Cor. 2:5-11).

2. The apostle wanted to give further instruction regarding the offering the Corinthians were raising for the poor saints at Jerusalem. "For as touching the ministering to the saints, it is superfluous for me to write to you: For I know the forwardness of your mind, for which I boast of you to them of Macedonia, that Achaia was ready a year ago; and your zeal hath provoked very many. Yet have I sent the brethren, lest our boasting of you should be in vain in this behalf; that, as I said, ye may be ready: Lest haply if they of Macedonia come with me, and find you unprepared, we (that we say not, ye) should be ashamed in this same confident boasting. Therefore I thought it necessary to exhort

the brethren, that they would go before unto you, and make up beforehand your bounty, whereof ye had notice before, that the same might be ready, as a matter of bounty, and not as of covetousness" (II Cor. 9:1-5).

3. Paul saw that there was further necessity for him to defend his apostleship against false teachers, who were seeking to establish themselves by criticizing him. "For his letters, say they, are weighty and powerful; but his bodily presence is weak, and his speech contemptible" (II Cor. 10:10). "For if he that cometh preacheth another Jesus, whom we have not preached, or if ye receive another spirit, which ye have not received, or another gospel, which ye have not accepted, ye might well bear with him" (11: 4). "For such are false apostles, deceitful workers, transforming themselves into the apostles of Christ. And no marvel; for Satan himself is transformed into an angel of light. Therefore it is no great thing if his ministers also be transformed as the ministers of righteousness; whose end shall be according to their works" (11:13-15). "Since ye seek a proof of Christ speaking in me . . ." (13:3).

The letter was evidently written not long after I Corinthians, probably in the latter part of

A.D. 57, and from some location in Macedonia. It is a magnificent treatise on "The True Gospel Ministry for Christ." Key verses are 4:5 and 5:20, 21: "For we preach not ourselves, but Christ Jesus the Lord; and ourselves your servants for Jesus' sake. . . . Now then we are ambassadors for Christ, as though God did beseech you by us; we pray you in Christ's stead, be ye reconciled to God. For he hath made him to be sin for us, who knew no sin; that we might be made the righteousness of God in him."

The word *ministry* in its various forms is used eighteen times in II Corinthians. The Greek word translated sometimes as *glory* and in other places as *boast* is used no less than twenty times. By this word comparison is made between that in which the false teacher *glories* (or *boasts*) and that in which the true minister of Christ glories. "But he that glorieth, let him glory in the Lord" (10:17). Chapters 1-7 concern the *Ministry of Reconciliation;* chapters 8, 9, the *Ministry of Giving;* and chapters 10-13, the *Ministry of the Apostle.*

Chapter Two

THE MINISTRY OF RECONCILIATION: PRINCIPLES OF A TRUE GOSPEL MINISTRY (chapters 1-7)

A. Introduction (1:1-11)

Paul, an apostle of Jesus Christ by the will of God, and Timothy our brother, unto the church of God which is at Corinth, with all the saints which are in all Achaia: Grace be to you and peace from God our Father, and from the Lord Jesus Christ" (1:1, 2). These opening verses contain the salutation of the apostle. In this letter he will again combat false teachers who cunningly questioned his authority. So he

13

begins by stating that he *is* an apostle, made so by Jesus Christ in accordance with the will of God the Father. In the greeting, Paul links with his own the name of his faithful helper Timothy, who was with him at the time of writing. It is made clear that he intended the letter to be read not only by the Corinthians but also by other Christians in the same area. *Achaia* was the name of the southern portion of what we now call Greece. *Macedonia* was the northern section.

Paul blesses them with his usual expressions of *grace* and *peace*. Authorities tell us that *grace* was a familiar Greek greeting, while the Jews then and today salute one another with the word *peace*. The apostle takes these familiar terms and invests them with a far greater depth of meaning than they had in ordinary speech. It is striking to note also that the name of the "Lord Jesus Christ" is linked on equal terms with that of "God our Father."

"Blessed be God, even the Father of our Lord Jesus Christ, the Father of mercies, and the God of all comfort; Who comforteth us in all our tribulation, that we may be able to comfort them which are in any trouble, by the comfort wherewith we ourselves are comforted of God.

For as the sufferings of Christ abound in us, so our consolation also aboundeth by Christ. And whether we be afflicted, it is for your consolation and salvation, which is effectual in the enduring of the same sufferings which we also suffer: or whether we be comforted, it is for your consolation and salvation. And our hope of you is steadfast, knowing, that as ye are partakers of the sufferings, so shall ye be also of the consolation" (1:3-7). Verses 3-11 contain Paul's *thanksgiving*, with verses 3-7 giving thanks for God's *comfort*. In these verses one Greek word is used no less than 10 times, but translated sometimes *comfort*, sometimes *consolation*. This word in the original language is closely related to the one used for the Holy Spirit in John 16:7— *Comforter*. The reference is to one who stands beside a person to support and strengthen him. Our God is "the God of all comfort." He is "the Father of mercies." *Father* is used here (and elsewhere in the Bible) idiomatically for the originator or source of a thing. Just as Satan is the source of all falsehood ("the father of lies"), so God is the source of all mercies.

The exact way in which God brings comfort to His children is not explicitly explained by the apostle. This is doubtless because He does it in various ways with various people. "The means by which the comfort was given Paul does not state. In the case of other Christians it comes sometimes by the reading of Scripture, sometimes by the removal of the affliction, sometimes by the secret offices of the divine Spirit. But, whatever the method, Paul traces the source of relief to the loving heart of God" (Charles R. Erdman, in *The Second Epistle of Paul to the Corinthians,* p. 21).

As we ourselves have tribulations and are comforted by God in them, then we are able better to help and console others in their afflictions. "The sufferings of Christ" (v. 5) are sufferings endured for the sake of Christ. While Paul especially refers to trials of that kind here, the teaching he gives can certainly be applied to any kind of sufferings God's children may be called on to endure. Though the sufferings *abound,* that is, go to great lengths, the comfort will also abound "by Christ."

Paul recognizes and acknowledges that his own sufferings are for the good of others, such as the Corinthians. They too are also entering now into the same sufferings for Christ. Paul and the other apostles are able to comfort them with the comfort they themselves have received. In it all his hope in them is "steadfast." He knows that since they are partaking of the sufferings of Christ, they will also partake of the consolation which God gives.

"For we would not, brethren, have you ignorant of our trouble which came to us in Asia, that we were pressed out of measure, above strength, insomuch that we despaired even of life: But we had the sentence of death in ourselves, that we should not trust in ourselves, but in God which raiseth the dead: Who delivered us from so great a death, and doth deliver: in whom we trust that he will yet deliver us; Ye also helping together by prayer for us, that for the gift bestowed upon us by the means of many persons thanks may be given by many on our behalf" (1:8-11). In these verses Paul expresses joy over God's *deliverance*. The *trouble* he speaks of (v. 8) refers either to the riot against Paul at Ephesus (see Acts 19:23), or to some other experience in that city about which we know nothing more. Some have speculated that the reference is to a serious physical illness, possibly connected with his "thorn in the flesh" which he mentions later (12:7). Whatever the experience may have been, it is plain that it was exceedingly trying, and it seems that the apostle

even became convinced that he would never live
through it.

But this "death sentence" was permitted so
that he would not depend on himself but rely
more fully on God who is able to do all things,
even raise the dead.   Whatever this serious affliction may have been, God both delivered Paul
and continued to grant deliverance to him.   The
apostle also gives very real credit to the Corinthians for this wonderful deliverance, because they
were holding him up in prayer.   Many bestowed
on him a good gift—the "gift" of intercessory
prayer.   Now many can rejoice in the gracious
answers to those petitions.

B. Affirmation of a Good Conscience (1:12-2:4)

Sometimes when unkind criticism is voiced, it
is better to bear it silently.   On other occasions
however, when false accusations if not answered
may damage a useful ministry for the Lord, it
is better to speak.   Because he had delayed an
intended visit, certain enemies of Paul accused
him of lightness and insincerity.   He now absolutely denies the charge, explaining that his delay
thus far has actually been for the purpose of
sparing them embarrassment.

"For our rejoicing is this, the testimony of
our conscience, that in simplicity and godly sincerity, not with fleshly wisdom, but by the grace
of God, we have had our conversation in the
world, and more abundantly to youward.   For
we write none other things unto you, than what
ye read or acknowledge; and I trust ye shall
acknowledge even to the end;   As also ye have
acknowledged us in part, that we are your rejoicing, even as ye also are ours in the day of the
Lord Jesus" (1:12-14).   With dignity the apostle
affirms that his own conscience is absolutely clear
in the matter (see Acts 23:1).   His dealing with
them all the way from the beginning has been
not "with fleshly wisdom" but rather with "simplicity and godly sincerity."   This has character-
ized his conduct with the entire world, and par-
ticularly with them.   In Corinth, as he reminded
them in his First Epistle, he ever sought to give
out the simple Gospel message in the power of
the Holy Spirit.   In Corinth he supplied his own
material needs by his personal labor.   That which
he writes to them now is no different from that
which he wrote previously which they acknowledged to be true.   He hopes that they will continue to acknowledge him to the end—that they
will rejoice in him and he in them "in the day

of Jesus Christ." This expression refers to the Rapture, when all believers must stand before Him.

"And in this confidence I was mindful to come unto you before, that ye might have a second benefit; And to pass by you into Macedonia, and to come again out of Macedonia unto you, and of you to be brought on my way toward Judaea. When I therefore was thus minded, did I use lightness? or the things that I purpose, do I purpose according to the flesh, that with me there should be yea yea, and nay nay?" (1:15-17). It had originally been the purpose of Paul to take the short route across the Aegean Sea from Ephesus to Corinth on his way to Macedonia. This design is mentioned in I Corinthians 16:5. It had probably been first told to them orally by Titus. Paul intended after completing his work in Macedonia to pass again through Corinth while on his way to Judaea. The Corinthians have now learned that he did not carry out that plan. Instead he went from Ephesus to Macedonia, passing them by. As a result, some of their number were accusing the apostle of "lightness" (or "fickleness," A.S.V.). Others were claiming that he was guilty of making fleshly plans outside the will of God, even that he was insincere, saying "yes yes," when he really meant "no no."

"But as God is true, our word toward you was not yea and nay. For the Son of God, Jesus. Christ, who was preached among you by us, even by me and Silvanus and Timotheus, was not yea and nay, but in him was yea. For all the promises of God in him are yea, and in him Amen, unto the glory of God by us" (1:18-20). Paul solemnly affirms that he has been completely honest with them and that these charges against him are utterly false. He reminds them that the Saviour whom he, Silas, and Timothy have preached among them was no insincere, fickle person. Jesus Christ is the great "Yes." He turns no one away, but satisfies every longing heart that comes to Him. "Him that cometh to me I will in no wise cast out. . . . He that cometh to me shall never hunger; and he that believeth on me shall never thirst" (John 6:37, 35). The Lord Jesus is the fulfiller of all the promises of God. The Corinthians well know that Paul's entire life has been devoted to the preaching of this all-faithful Christ. Is it possible that a man who so preaches such a Saviour could himself be fickle and insincere? Thus the apostle argues from his preaching to his personal character.

"Now he which stablisheth us with you in Christ, and hath anointed us, is God; Who hath also sealed us, and given the earnest of the Spirit in our hearts" (1:21, 22). Paul continues to insist that he is not hypocritical, but that his life is "stablished" (made firm) by God. This is true not only of himself but of other Christians too— God has stablished "us with you." Believers are "anointed." As the holy oil was poured on prophets, priests, and kings of old to signify their empowering for service, so the Holy Spirit has come upon us. This took place at the time we believed on the Lord Jesus Christ. The Holy Spirit has also "sealed" us. A *seal* is used to denote several different things: a finished transaction, a mark of ownership, a guarantee of safe delivery. All these things are true of Christians. So then Paul bears the seal of God, and he *could not* be light and insincere.

"Moreover I call God for a record upon my soul, that to spare you I came not as yet unto Corinth. Not for that we have dominion over your faith, but are helpers of your joy: for by faith ye stand" (1:23, 24). No, the real reason why Paul did not come to Corinth as he had originally planned was due to a desire to "spare" them. Since they had not corrected the things

that were wrong, if he had come he would have
had to exercise severe discipline among them,
which would of course have grieved them. Immediately following this statement however he
hastens to show that he does not mean that he
considers himself a sort of "boss" or "pope"
over their faith. *Faith* is a very personal matter
between the individual soul and God. "By faith
ye stand."   Paul's place—and that of all true
Christian ministers—is not to lord it over others
(I Peter 5:2, 3), but rather to help their brethren to the position in which they can experience
the full joy God wants them to have.

"But I determined this with myself, that I
would not come again to you in heaviness. For
if I make you sorry, who is he then that maketh
me glad, but the same which is made sorry by
me? And I wrote this same unto you, lest, when
I came, I should have sorrow from them of whom
I ought to rejoice; having confidence in you all,
that my joy is the joy of you all. For out of much
affliction and anguish of heart I wrote unto you
with many tears; not that ye should be grieved,
but that ye might know the love which I have
more abundantly unto you" (2:1-4). The apostle
now explains more fully the reason why he has
not made a second visit to them. His first de-

sire had been to come immediately. His final
decision was that he would not visit them at a
time when he would have to come "in heaviness,"
or literally, in *grief*, and "make them sorry" by
the necessary use of stern discipline. His words
in verse 2 might be paraphrased: "I should expect you to make me glad, but how can you if I
in advance make you sorry and grieve you?"

When he visits them, he wants to receive joy
from them as well as to give them joy, so his
delay was largely for the purpose of allowing
them time to correct their own errors. Since
Paul says: "I determined . . . that I would not
come *again* to you in heaviness," some readers
have thought that the *again* indicates that he had
already made a second sorrowful visit to Corinth.
However such a visit is not mentioned elsewhere.
"The meaning is *not* 'that I would not pay you a
second, sad visit,' but 'that *my second visit to you
should not be a sad one*' " *(Pulpit Commentary,*
Vol. 19, p. 36).

Verse 4 reveals in a touching way the spirit in
which Paul wrote First Corinthians. These words
give us a significant insight which we would
otherwise know nothing about. His previous rebukes, which in black and white sound quite
stern, were written "with many tears." Thus it

should ever be with the true servant of Christ when on occasion he has to reprove and rebuke (see II Tim. 4:2). This makes it clear that Paul's previous letter had been written not simply to shame the Corinthians and put them to grief, but rather was an overflowing of the tender love and affection he had for them.

C. Appeal for the Repentant Offender (2:5-13)

"But if any have caused grief, he hath not grieved me, but in part: that I may not overcharge you all. Sufficient to such a man is this punishment, which was inflicted of many. So that contrariwise ye ought rather to forgive him, and comfort him, lest perhaps such a one should be swallowed up with overmuch sorrow. Wherefore I beseech you that ye would confirm your love toward him. For to this end also did I write, that I might know the proof of you, whether ye be obedient in all things" (2:5-9). It seems obvious that the apostle is in these words referring to the offending church member previously mentioned in I Corinthians 5. The important point was not so much that this unhappy case had grieved Paul, but that it was a sorrow and a hindrance to the entire church. In verse 5 the expression "in part" properly goes with "you all." "He hath caused sorrow, not to me, but in part (that I press not too heavily) to you all" (A.S.V.).

The Corinthians had been told: "Put away from among yourselves that wicked person" (I Cor. 5:13). This discipline had been effected by the many members of the church. But now that the offender is truly sorry for his sin, he should be forgiven. His brethren should confirm their love toward him by forgiving and restoring him to fellowship. When the apostle had asked that the guilty party be dealt with, he had desired to learn if they would be obedient. Now he urges that forgiveness be granted if they feel that there is true repentance.

"To whom ye forgive anything, I forgive also: for if I forgave anything, to whom I forgave it, for your sakes forgave I it in the person of Christ; Lest Satan should get an advantage of us; for we are not ignorant of his devices" (2:10, 11). If the members of the Corinthian church forgive, then Paul will forgive also, as in the very living presence of Christ. In dealing with such matters Christians must be exceedingly careful lest Satan "get an advantage of them." By this particular incident some of Satan's *devices* (original word means a "thought out plan") are brought to light: (1) He seeks to tempt Christians through the lust of the flesh in the hope that they will ruin their lives and spoil their testimony through fleshly passions. (2) When backsliding Christians realize their condition and feel repentant, the Devil seeks to keep them down by leading them to think that their case is hopeless. He tells them that they have gone too far and that it is too late to return to the Lord. (3) In the case of a church, Satan tries to get the people to go to either of two extremes—to be too lax, too tolerant of evil, or too severe, hard, cold, pharisaical.

"Furthermore, when I came to Troas to preach Christ's gospel, and a door was opened unto me of the Lord, I had no rest in my spirit, because I found not Titus my brother: but taking my leave of them, I went from thence into Macedonia" (2:12, 13). In these words, Paul recalls his visit to Troas after leaving Ephesus. There seemed to be excellent opportunities there, but he found himself unable to take full advantage of them due to his sadness at not having heard from Titus. The latter had evidently previously arranged to meet the apostle at Troas with a report on conditions at Corinth. Paul then journeyed on to Macedonia expecting to meet his young co-worker there, since they had missed the previous connection. Later, in chapter 7, that meeting is described. But now the inspired writer turns to the main theme of his great epistle —the glorious nature of the true Gospel ministry.

D. The First Characteristic of the True Gospel Ministry: Continual Triumph as We Make Manifest the Sweetness of God's Knowledge (2:14-17)

"Now thanks be unto God, which always causeth us to triumph in Christ, and maketh manifest the savor of his knowledge by us in every place. For we are unto God a sweet savor of Christ, in them that are saved, and in them that perish: To the one we are the savor of death unto death; and to the other the savor of life unto life. And who is sufficient for these things? For we are not as many, which corrupt the word of God: but as of sincerity, but as of God, in the sight of God speak we in Christ."

In this portion of the epistle, the thought centers around a graphic figure which was doubtless familiar to the early Christians. "There is no question that the figure Paul employed in this verse is that of a Roman triumph" (Morgan, in *The Corinthian Letters of Paul,* page 235).

"When a Roman general had been out into some distant land to put down an uprising, or to win new lands for the Roman empire, to defeat great armies, the senate frequently voted him 'a triumph.' When he and his army returned to Rome a public holiday was declared, and all the people thronged to the main thoroughfare to see this general enter in triumph. Here is a long line of captives, representatives of the people he has subjugated. They are in chains, and are holding censers in their hands, and sweet, fragrant incense arises. Then comes the general, and behind him another long line of captives bearing censers. These in front are to be set at liberty, and the fragrant incense is the odor of life unto them. Those behind are condemned to die, and are going on to the arena; they are to be thrown to the wild beasts or put to death in some other way, and the fragrant incense that arises from their censers is a savor of death. The general marches on in triumph. There are some with a savor of life, there are others with a savor of death" (Ironside, in *Addresses on the Second Epistle to the Corinthians,* pp. 61, 62).

The thought then is not merely that God "causeth us to triumph" as the Authorized Version renders it, but that God "leadeth us in triumph" (A.S.V.). It is clear that in this picture Christ is the victorious leader. But *we* are not represented as His conquered captives, as many expositors seem to think. "The thought is not either that Paul is made a victor or that he is exhibited as a captive, but that God associates him in the divine triumph of His redeeming work" (Erdman, op. cit., p. 35).

Through the lives of His true witnesses, the Lord makes known the sweet savor of His knowledge. This fragrant perfume arising from our testimony for Him falls however on two entirely different groups. Those who *reject* the Gospel find this testimony to be a "savor of death unto death." To them it seems a childish message about a remote Man who lived and died in the distant past. But on the other hand to those who *receive* the Gospel it becomes a "savor of life unto life," a life-giving message concerning a living vital Saviour.

As the apostle considers the terrific importance of this message, which it is our responsibility to bring to men, and the eternal destiny of souls which is involved in its reception or rejection,

he utters the heartfelt cry: "Who is sufficient
for these things?" Surely every true Christian
has experienced something of the same feeling.

Paul's immediate answer is however a bit sur-
prising. We would expect him to say that none
of us is sufficient in himself. This answer is
given later (3:5). But at the present moment
Paul shows that the many *false* teachers who corrupt the Word of God (by mixing falsehood
with truth) are certainly *not* sufficient for the
solemnity of the occasion. Those however who
speak the Word of God in *sincerity,* "in Christ"
—and those alone—are sufficient to meet the ap-
palling situation we face.

E. A True Gospel Ministry Proves Itself by Changed
Lives (3:1-5)

"Do we begin again to commend ourselves?
or need we, as some others, epistles of commendation to you, or letters of commendation from
you? Ye are our epistle written in our hearts,
known and read of all men: Forasmuch as ye
are manifestly declared to be the epistle of Christ
ministered by us, written not with ink, but with
the Spirit of the living God; not in tables of
stone, but in fleshy tables of the heart. And such

trust have we through Christ to Godward: Not
that we are sufficient of ourselves to think anything as of ourselves; but our sufficiency is of
God."

It is evident that some of his critics had accused
Paul of boasting about himself. His manner of
speaking in the closing verse of chapter 2 now
leads him to quickly say: "Do we begin again to
commend ourselves?" No, he is *not* praising
himself. Neither does he need to have letters of
commendation either to or from Corinth, as some
have sought to secure. The very lives of the
Corinthians are a sufficient testimony to the ef-
ficacy of the apostolic work Paul had wrought
among them. Their changed lives can be seen
by all. Although not all will listen, praise God
that whenever the Gospel is given out in the
power of the Holy Spirit, souls will be saved
and lives will be changed.

In 2:3 Paul amplifies his illustration to its full
extent. The "author" of these living epistles is
Christ, the *pen* is Paul, the spiritual *ink* is the
Holy Spirit. The wonderful thing about these
"epistles" is that they are not written on tablets
of stone as were the Ten Commandments, but
on "fleshy tables of the heart." The apostle
states that "such trust" he has, that is, that the

changed lives of his converts are sufficient commendation for his ministry. The one who inspires such confidence in him, in relation to
God, is Christ.

When Paul claimed a bit earlier to be "sufficient" he did not at all mean that he was sufficient in himself to work for Christ, or even to
judge his own labor. "Not that we are sufficient
of ourselves to think anything as of ourselves."
The Greek verb here translated "to think" means
"to take account of something." Paul's sufficiency
—and that of all true Gospel ministers—is "of
God."

F. The True Gospel Ministry Is Far More Glorious Than
That of the Old Covenant (3:6-18)

Paul's reference in verse 3 to "tables of stone"
was not by any means accidental. At Corinth
and elsewhere his chief opponents were the
Judaizers who proudly undertook the task of being ministers of the Old Covenant. Although
professing to be followers of Jesus Christ, they
exalted the law of Moses. They insisted that a
person could *not* be saved simply by faith in
Christ alone but that it was absolutely necessary

to keep the whole law (see Acts 15:1, 24). In other words they attempted to *combine* law and grace.

The apostle Paul writes: God "also hath made us able ministers of the new testament; not of the letter, but of the spirit: for the letter killeth, but the spirit giveth life" (3:6). The true Gospel minister is *not* a minister of the Old Covenant. He is rather an "able minister of the New Covenant" (cf. Matt. 26:28). No longer are we under the Old Covenant but, thank God, under the New. The contrast drawn between the "letter" and the "spirit" is not at all between the literal and the figurative methods of interpreting Scripture, but between the law and grace. Under the Old Covenant of law men were condemned—killed. The law told them of their sin but gave them no power to live victoriously over it. Under the New Covenant the Spirit of God comes to dwell in the heart of the believer, producing new life and providing new power, by means of which sin can be vanquished.

"But if the ministration of death, written and engraven in stones, was glorious, so that the children of Israel could not steadfastly behold the face of Moses for the glory of his countenance; which glory was to be done away: How shall not the ministration of the spirit be rather glorious? For if the ministration of condemnation be glory, much more doth the ministration of righteousness exceed in glory" (3:7-9). The service of Moses in bringing the law of God to the people of Israel is described as "glorious." The glory of the law was manifested by the fact that the very face of Moses shone when he descended from Mount Sinai to present God's statutes to the Israelites (cf. Exod. 34:29, 30). But as time passed, the glory on the face of Moses gradually disappeared and was eventually "done away." This was an illustration of the fact that the law itself was not a permanent system but was in due time to pass away. Glorious though it was, the law was a "ministration of death"—it condemned all men as guilty sinners. If it possessed a certain glory, even though a ministration of death and a temporary system, how much more glorious is the "ministration of the Spirit," such as Paul had. Instead of condemning sinful men it offers righteousness and the Holy Spirit as a free gift.

"For even that which was made glorious had no glory in this respect, by reason of the glory that excelleth. For if that which is done away was glorious, much more that which remaineth is glorious. Seeing then that we have such hope, we use great plainness of speech: And not as Moses, which put a veil over his face, that the children of Israel could not steadfastly look to the end of that which is abolished: But their minds were blinded: for until this day remaineth the same veil untaken away in the reading of the old testament; which veil is done away in Christ. But even unto this day, when Moses is read, the veil is upon their heart. Nevertheless when it shall turn to the Lord, the veil shall be taken away" (3:10-16).

The law, which was *made* glorious, had no *real* splendor when compared with the glory of the dispensation of grace. The latter possesses "the glory that excelleth." However if the law, although temporary, had a certain glory of its own, how much more glorious is the Gospel of God's grace which "remaineth" (or "abideth"). Since Paul and other Gospel preachers "have such hope"—hope in a Gospel message whose glory will never fade—they have nothing to hide but speak with "plainness" (or "boldness"). They have nothing to conceal, as Moses hid his face from the Israelites so that they might not see the glory fade away.

Due to the familiar Authorized Version translation of Exodus 34:33, English readers for several centuries have labored under the misconception that Moses put the veil upon his face *to keep the people from seeing the glory*, whereas Paul clearly brings out here, Moses put on the veil *after* he had spoken *to keep them from seeing the glory pass away*. The American Standard Version translates Exodus 34:33: "And when Moses had done speaking with them, he put a veil on his face."

Sad to say, the people of Israel as a whole failed to understand the lesson taught by this symbolism. They thought the law was permanent, and they failed to see the greater glory which Messiah would bring. So to this day, when the Old Testament is read, that same veil of blindness, prejudice, and unbelief hangs over their hearts. They ignore the many passages in the Old Testament which should lead them to Jesus Christ.

In the last part of verse 14 ("which veil is done away in Christ") the word *veil* is printed in the King James Version in italics, a device which indicates that the original text of Scripture had no such corresponding word, but that it was added by the translators. In this case it is deceptive and should be omitted in order that the true meaning may be understood. "It is not the veil, but the Old Covenant, which is being done away in Christ" *(Pulpit Commentary, op. cit.,* p. 61).

So "even unto this day" when the law of Moses is read the hearts of the Israelites are still blinded to its true implications. But when their hearts are ready to turn to the Lord, that veil will be taken away. And that that day will eventually come many prophecies give assurance, among them Romans 11:25, 26: "For I would not, brethren, that ye should be ignorant of this mystery, lest ye should be wise in your own conceits; that blindness in part is happened to Israel, until the fullness of the Gentiles be come in. And so all Israel shall be saved: as it is written, There shall come out of Sion the Deliverer, and shall turn away ungodliness from Jacob."

"Now the Lord is that Spirit: and where the Spirit of the Lord is, there is liberty. But we all, with open face beholding as in a glass the glory of the Lord, are changed into the same image from glory to glory, even as by the Spirit of the Lord" (3:17, 18). The Lord Jesus is said to be "that Spirit." The direct reference is to verse 6; He is "the Spirit who gives life" in contrast to "the letter" of the law which brings death.

He is referred to in similar manner in I Corinthians 15:45: "And so it is written, The first man Adam was made a living soul; the last Adam was made a quickening spirit." Where the Spirit of the Lord gives life there is true *liberty*, freedom from the bondage of the law, freedom to truly serve God. "For if the blood of bulls and of goats, and the ashes of an heifer sprinkling the unclean, sanctifieth to the purifying of the flesh: How much more shall the blood of Christ, who through the eternal Spirit offered himself without spot to God, purge your conscience from dead works to serve the living God?" (Heb. 9:13, 14). All who know Christ are even now beholding "the glory of the Lord." This we do with "open face" (or, literally, "unveiled face"). This again reminds us of Moses, for Exodus 34:34 says: "But when Moses went in before the Lord to speak with him, he took the veil off, until he came out. And he came out and spake unto the children of Israel that which he was commanded." At present we do not see the Lord directly, but "as in a glass" (or "mirror"). This mirror is the Word of God. As we continue to behold Him we are "being changed" (present tense) even as Moses was changed. But our change is not just a temporary transformation on the outside, as was Moses', but a *transfiguration* from the inside, which will not fade away.

G. The Message of the True Gospel Ministry (4:1-6)

"Therefore seeing we have this ministry, as we have received mercy, we faint not; But have renounced the hidden things of dishonesty, not walking in craftiness, nor handling the word of God deceitfully; but by manifestation of the truth commending ourselves to every man's conscience in the sight of God. But if our gospel be hid, it is hid to them that are lost: In whom the god of this world hath blinded the minds of them which believe not, lest the light of the glorious gospel of Christ, who is the image of God, should shine unto them. For we preach not ourselves, but Christ Jesus the Lord; and ourselves your servants for Jesus' sake. For God, who commanded the light to shine out of darkness, hath shined in our hearts, to give the light of the knowledge of the glory of God in the face of Jesus Christ."

Paul now gives a further answer to his critics who had accused him of dishonesty and deceit. At the same time he shows in a positive way just

what the message of the true Gospel ministry is.
The *ministry* he refers to in the opening verse
of the chapter is that of 3:8, 9—"the ministration
of the spirit," "the ministration of righteousness."
Ever remembering the mercy of God, the true
Gospel minister does not lose courage. He has
openly and sincerely renounced the "hidden
things of shame." He has turned away from
craftiness, from all underhanded tricky dealing. He
does not handle God's Word *deceitfully;* he is
not like the "many, which corrupt the Word of
God" (2:17). Those who handle the Bible deceitfully either do so by adding to it false teaching (like that mentioned in I Cor. 15:12), or by
wresting Scripture out of its plain and true significance to make people think it means something altogether different from what it really
teaches (see II Peter 3:16).

The true minister however gives out faithfully
the truth of God, and by his straightforward
sincere dealing "commends himself" to the consciences of those who hear him. In a word, he
serves as in the presence of God Himself. But
then, if the true minister of the Gospel, such as
Paul, so clearly manifests forth the Gospel, why
do some fail to understand it? The reason is
that men refuse to *believe* the Gospel. They will-

fully turn away from it and Satan then blinds their minds to its beauty and power. Satan, it should be carefully observed, is "the god of this age." Whether they realize it or not, unsaved people actually serve and worship him. The Devil does not want the Gospel light to shine in the hearts of men.

This wonderful Gospel concerns the glory of Christ. Christ is "the image of God" (v. 4). By comparison with Hebrews 10:1 it will be seen that *image* means the real, solid substance of something. Jesus Christ said: "He that hath seen me hath seen the Father" (John 14:9). So then the message of the true Gospel minister is the *truth* of God, the Gospel of the glory of Christ. The real minister does not preach himself (as the false teacher usually does), but he preaches "Christ Jesus the Lord." For the sake of Jesus, he himself takes the place of a servant to all. Even as God, on the first day of creation, brought light into darkness (Gen. 1:1-5), so the Lord shines in the heart of the one who believes the Gospel, revealing to him "the knowledge of the glory of God." This glory is to be found "in the face of Jesus Christ." "Probably, however, there is a reference to the glory of God, not as *reflected* from the face of Christ, but as concentrated in and beaming from it" *(Pulpit Commentary, op. cit.,* p. 90).

H. The Power of the True Gospel Ministry (4:7-15)

"But we have this treasure in earthen vessels, that the excellency of the power may be of God, and not of us" (4:7). The true Gospel minister possesses this *treasure*—the light of the knowledge of the glory of God—in an "earthen vessel." This term refers to the human body and the human nature which are at best very weak. It is said that ancient peoples often hid their treasure of gold or jewels in earthenware vessels. It may be that the apostle had in mind also the lights which Gideon's men had hidden within their pitchers (Judg. 7). When the pitchers were broken, the lights shone forth and the enemy was defeated. So the Christian endures suffering in the flesh while letting the light of Christ shine forth from his life. All this is done in order that it may be seen that the glorious power of the Gospel is altogether "of God and not of us."

"We are troubled on every side, yet not distressed; we are perplexed, but not in despair;

Persecuted, but not forsaken; cast down, but not destroyed; Always bearing about in the body the dying of the Lord Jesus that the life also of Jesus might be made manifest in our body. For we which live are always delivered unto death for Jesus' sake, that the life also of Jesus might be made manifest in our mortal flesh. So then death worketh in us, but life in you" (4:8-12). With these striking words, the apostle shows how weak these earthen vessels are, and yet, at the same time, how wonderfully they are sustained by God's power. "To contrast his own weakness with the power of God, Paul suddenly changes the figure of speech. He pictures himself as a soldier in the most dire straits, yet ever delivered by divine grace. With a few strokes of the pen he describes the successive states of a battle. The warrior is surrounded, hard pressed, driven from the field, struck by the enemy's sword, given over to death, yet marvelously rescued by an unseen Friend" (Erdman, *op. cit.*, p. 47).

We are "troubled on every side." The original language signifies "hemmed in" on every side, yet at the same time not "cramped." We are "perplexed, but not in despair"—literally, "at a loss but not utterly at a loss." We are "persecuted, but not forsaken." The Greek text here

has in it the picture of being pursued by enemies
but not left to their power. We are "cast down,
but not destroyed." "This carries on the previous
figure. Though the pursuers overtake and smite
down, yet we are not killed" (Vincent, in *Word
Studies in the New Testament,* Vol. 3, p. 313).
Verse 10 is explained by verse 11. Paul and his
friends were always in imminent danger of being
slain by their foes, even as Christ was, yet on many
occasions they were wonderfully delivered by the
Lord, so that they might continue to bear testimony to Him (Acts 23:11). So then, says the
apostle, "death works in us" (as he has just been
describing), so that *life* may work in others, like
the Corinthians, as he ministers the Gospel to
them.

"We having the same spirit of faith, according
as it is written, I believed, and therefore have
I spoken; we also believe, and therefore speak;
Knowing that he which raised up the Lord Jesus
shall raise up us also by Jesus, and shall present
us with you. For all things are for your sakes,
that the abundant grace might through the
thanksgiving of many redound to the glory of
God" (4:13-15). The apostle is willing to suffer such trials because he has the same spirit of

faith which the psalmist possessed when he wrote
Psalm 116:10, which is here quoted. Surely the
same should be true of every Gospel minister and
witness. Anyone who does not really believe what
he says should not speak at all. Paul *does* believe. Even though in the end his enemies may
finally take his life, yet he has confidence that
the same God who raised up the Lord Jesus will
some day likewise raise from the dead all who
are in Christ and will present them to Him as a
bride is presented to the bridegroom. So actually all the things he endures are for the sake of
his converts, that as they experience God's
"abundant grace" their thanksgiving might "redound" ("abound," A.S.V.) to the "'glory of
God."

I. The Hope of the True Gospel Ministry (4:16-5:10)

"For which cause we faint not; but though our
outward man perish, yet the inward man is renewed day by day. For our light affliction, which
is but for a moment, worketh for us a far more
exceeding and eternal weight of glory; While we
look not at the things which are seen, but at the
things which are not seen: for the things which

are seen are temporal; but the things which are not seen are eternal" (4:16-18).

Because we know that God is with us to bless and to deliver, we do not "faint," or *lose courage.* Our "outward man" is of course the physical body with its weakness and infirmities. As we go on through life it gradually is perishing. Our "inward man" is the soul, or spirit. As we walk with the Lord, that is constantly being "renewed" day by day (cf. III John 2). We can think of our present affliction as "light" and "for a moment" in comparison with the "weight of glory" that lies ahead of us in eternity. His own "light affliction" Paul will later graphically describe in 11:23-29! The present affliction is going to bring about for us this "exceeding glory." But we will not view it from this perspective if we are looking at *the things which are seen,* if our minds are centered on the visible things of this present world. Instead we are to keep our eyes on *the things which are not seen.* These are eternal while the things of this world are transitory. What, by the way, are these "eternal things"? Christ the Saviour, God the Father, the Holy Spirit, Heaven, eternal life, salvation in Christ, and many others. These are the truly abiding things.

"For we know that if our earthly house of
this tabernacle were dissolved, we have a building of God, a house not made with hands, eternal
in the heavens.   For in this we groan, earnestly
desiring to be clothed upon with our house which
is from heaven: If so be that being clothed we
shall not be found naked.   For we that are in
this tabernacle do groan, being burdened: not
for that we would be unclothed, but clothed upon, that mortality might be swallowed up of life"
(5:1-4) .

It is evident that the apostle Paul had physical
weaknesses which made him realize keenly that
his "outward man" was perishing.   Yet he is confident that even if it falls to his lot to have "this
tabernacle" altogether "dissolved" by death, yet
he still has a heavenly building to look forward
to, a resurrection body which will endure forever.   This resurrection body is not like human
buildings which are "made with hands" but is
God-made.   Therefore, realizing the weakness of
the present body, he and other Christians "groan"
as they longingly anticipate that wonderful resurrection body.   The thing for which we groan is
not death and the dissolution of the body.   We
do not long to be "unclothed," so to speak, but
rather to be "clothed upon," to have our mortal

bodies transformed and perfected *without* dying at the time of the Rapture (I Thess. 4:17; I Cor. 15:51, 52). Then our bodies, as well as our souls, will become immortal.

It has been suggested that in this section Paul is referring to some sort of intermediate body, which the believer will possess *between* death and the resurrection. It hardly seems that such a body could be called *eternal* (v. 1). No, Paul evidently here refers to the resurrection body believers will receive when Christ comes again. As to the period between death and the resurrection not a great deal is revealed. In this present chapter (also in Phil. 1:23) we are told however that the Christian, when he departs this life goes to be with Christ, and his condition is immediately "far better" than that on the present earth. But it will be still more wonderful when the glorious resurrection comes.

Some have imagined that because Paul says "we" in I Thessalonians 4:15 he felt sure that Christ was going to return during his own life-time. It might just as well be argued from II Corinthians 5:1 that Paul expected to die *before* Christ came, because again he says "we." The fact is that Paul, like ourselves, did not know which it would be. Near the end of his life, God apparently showed him that he must die (see II Tim. 4:6).

"Now he that hath wrought us for the selfsame thing is God, who also hath given unto us the earnest of the Spirit. Therefore we are always confident, knowing that, whilst we are at home in the body, we are absent from the Lord: (For we walk by faith, not by sight:) We are confident, I say, and willing rather to be absent from the body, and to be present with the Lord. Wherefore we labor, that, whether present or absent, we may be accepted of him. For we must all appear before the judgment seat of Christ; that every one may receive the things done in his body, according to that he hath done, whether it be good or bad" (5:5-10).

God has worked in us, by saving and leading us on in the Christian life, for the very purpose of which Paul has just been writing—our future glorified state. Meanwhile, as an assurance that He will fulfill this promise of future glory, He has even now given us the Holy Spirit as an earnest. We are therefore always of good courage since we know that while we are still in the body here on this earth we are "absent from the Lord." Of course in a spiritual way He is with us, but we are not now personally in His pres-

ence in the glory land. Even so if we must die
and leave the body, we will be personally present
with the Lord in Heaven. For this reason we
"labor"—or, as in the literal Greek, *we are am-
bitious*—whether still in the body when He comes
again, or whether it is our lot to pass through
the experience of death, that either way we may
be well-pleasing to Him at His advent.   The
cause of our great ambition in this respect—to
be pleasing to Him at the time of His coming—
is that *all* of us must then stand before His *judgment seat*. Works done in this life will there be
tested. Rewards will be given out. (For more
information on this important scene, see I Cor.
3:11-15.)

J. The Motives of the True Gospel Ministry (5:11-16)

"Knowing therefore the terror of the Lord, we
persuade men; but we are made manifest unto
God; and I trust also are made manifest in your
consciences. For we commend not ourselves again
unto you, but give you occasion to glory on our
behalf, that ye may have somewhat to answer
them which glory in appearance, and not in heart.
For whether we be beside ourselves, it is to God:

or whether we be sober, it is for your cause" (5: 11-13).

The fact that "we must all appear before the judgment seat of Christ" leads the apostle to tell of the first motive of the true Gospel ministry. This motive is "the fear of the Lord." The Greek word here used refers to "reverential fear of God, as a controlling motive of the life, in matters spiritual and moral, not a mere fear of His power and righteous retribution, but a wholesome dread of displeasing Him, a fear which banishes the terror that shrinks from His presence (Rom. 8: 15), and which influences the disposition and attitude of one whose circumstances are guided by trust in God" (W. E. Vine, in *Expository Dictionary of New Testament Words,* p. 84). One well-known Bible teacher tells of a time in his early life when he carefully avoided any place where he might hear God's Word or meet Him. Knowing himself a guilty sinner, he feared to come *into* God's presence. Finally there came a day when he received Christ as Saviour and trusted in Him for salvation. Since then he fears the Lord, but in a different way. Now he fears lest he get *out* of God's presence and will. In the light of such a fear the true Gospel minister persuades men to turn to God.

Though some may attack and criticize him, Paul needs no defense before God who knows his true motives. He also trusts that he needs no defense before the Corinthians. He does not intend to praise himself, but simply wishes to tell what the Lord has done both for and through him. In this the Corinthians can "glory" (or *boast*), when they have to answer the apostle's critics. These opponents boast of that which is external and superficial (like human wisdom) rather than in that which is deep and abiding.

Some of Paul's enemies had evidently accused him of madness. Others had accused him of being just the opposite, of being "sober," of having "a method in his madness." If the first be true, says Paul, "it is to God." If the latter, "it is for your cause."

"For the love of Christ constraineth us; because we thus judge, that if one died for all, then were all dead: And that he died for all, that they which live should not henceforth live unto themselves, but unto him which died for them, and rose again. Wherefore henceforth know we no man after the flesh: yea, though we have known Christ after the flesh, yet now henceforth know we him no more" (5:14-16).

The second grand motive of the true Gospel

ministry is "the love of Christ." This expression
could grammatically refer either to *our* love for
Him, or to *His* love for us. In this case there is
really no difference in the two. If the reference
is actually to *His* love for us, then the thought is
that this inspires *our* love for Him. The last part
of verse 14 is better rendered: "We thus judge,
that one died for all, therefore all died" (A.S.V.).
The one who died for all men is of course the
Lord Jesus Christ. He did this so effectively that
it can be truly said that in Him "all died." The
work He accomplished was not only for the purpose of paying the *penalty* of our sin, but also
that we might have *new life* in Him. We who
believe are joined with Him not in His death
alone but also in His resurrection life. No more
are we to live just for self. Now we live "unto
Christ."

So then, no longer do we know any man "after
the flesh." "And so we now look out upon the
world through altogether different eyes from
those we used when we belonged to it. When
men of the world, we made much of the flesh,
and all that was linked with it. We thought of
men as great, or as rich, or as powerful, talented
or able, as superior to one another. Some men
we despised because they were poor and ignorant,

and degraded, with little intelligence, and less talented, but now all that is changed. . . . We look out now upon this world, not thinking of the different distinctions between man and man, but as seeing a world of sinners for whom Christ died, and we realize that all men, whether rich or poor, foolish or wise, whether barbarian or civilized, whether morons or highly talented, are dear to the heart of God. . . . So in touch with Christ Himself, we are prepared to suffer, to give, to deny ourselves, we are prepared to die, if need be, in order to bring others to a saving knowledge of this redemption which means so much to us   (Ironside, *op. cit.,* p. 146, 147).

Not even do we know "Christ after the flesh." This means that we do not think of Him simply as He was in His earthly life in Palestine many years ago. No, we know Him as He is now— risen and glorified. It is to this glorious risen Christ we are joined!

K. The Nature of the True Gospel Ministry (5:17-21)

"Therefore if any man be in Christ, he is a new creature: old things are passed away; behold, all things are become new. And all things are of

God, who hath reconciled us to himself by Jesus
Christ, and hath given to us the ministry of reconciliation; To wit, that God was in Christ, reconciling the world unto himself, not imputing their
trespasses unto them; and hath committed unto
us the word of reconciliation. Now then we are
ambassadors for Christ, as though God did beseech
you by us: we pray you in Christ's stead, be ye
reconciled to God. For he hath made him to be
sin for us, who knew no sin; that we might be
made the righteousness of God in him" (5:17-
21).

The Gospel ministry is therefore a service of
bringing lost men to Christ, so that in Him they
may find new life. The one who is "in Christ"
becomes "a new creation." The things of the
old life pass away. A new life is given. All this
is "of God." Through Jesus Christ He has "reconciled" us. To *reconcile* is to bring back into
proper adjustment. Theologians sometimes use
it of God. The New Testament never uses it of
Him, but only of man. The Bible never speaks
of God being reconciled, but of man being reconciled to God. God was never out of adjustment and never needed to be brought back into
right relations. Man was and is out of adjust-

ment and does need to be brought back into proper relationship with God.

After each one of us is individually and personally brought back into adjustment with God, then He gives to us the privilege of telling others. This is "the ministry of reconciliation." The *message* of reconciliation is that "God was in Christ reconciling the world unto himself." Jesus Christ was more than a human being—He was God in the flesh. He said, "I and my Father are one" (John 10:30); "Believest thou not that I am in the Father, and the Father in me? the words that I speak unto you I speak not of myself: but the Father that dwelleth in me, he doeth the works" (John 14:10). By His work He atoned for all men. He "reconciled the world" unto God, so that the sins of men would not be *imputed* (or reckoned). This task has already been accomplished for all people. The Gospel minister now serves as an "ambassador for Christ." An *ambassador* is a high minister of state who represents one country, or sovereign, in another land. We now represent God, and in the place of Christ, who has returned to Heaven, we say to those who are not believers: "Be ye reconciled to God." This means, in other words, receive the work Christ has already wrought for you, so that you

may in a real and personal way be brought back
into adjustment with God.

The *reason* men can be reconciled to God is
because the Father has made the Son to be "sin
for us." This does not mean He became sinful
Himself. Quite the contrary—"He knew no sin.'
It does mean that on Calvary's cross He took our
place and bore our sin. All this He did so that
we, who are in ourselves but guilty sinners, might
"become the righteousness of God in Him."

All that is His is imputed to me.
　O, lovely and fair is my Lord,
And He gives me the robe of His own righteousness
　To cover my sins, says His Word.

All that I am is imputed to Him.
　O, black were my shame and my guilt
Which were laid upon Him on Calvary's cross,
　But precious His blood that was spilt.

Was ever a bargain so wondrous as this?
　O, matchless His love and His grace!
My guilt for His glory, my pain for His peace,
　My night for the light of His face!"

　　　　　　　　　　　　—AUTHOR UNKNOWN

L. The Trials of the True Gospel Ministry (6:1-10)

"We then, as workers together with him, beseech you also that ye receive not the grace of God in vain. (For he saith, I have heard thee in a time accepted, and in the day of salvation have I succored thee: behold, now is the accepted time; behold, now is the day of salvation.) Giving no offense in anything, that the ministry be not blamed" (6:1-3).

Paul now undertakes to show the trials that ambassadors for Christ, such as himself, must endure. The King James Version (also A.S.V.) adds in verse 1 the words "with him." These words are in italics, indicating they were not in the original Greek text. They are best omitted. Such ambassadors are not exactly "workers together with him." Only Christ is truly a "fellow worker with God." God's human servants are fellow workers *with one another,* urging men and women not to receive "the grace of God in vain." "This they might do by failing to accept and appropriate this grace, by refusing the gospel Paul proclaimed, or by not so living as to show that they had accepted the grace of God in Christ and were constrained by His love" (Erdman, *op. cit.,* p. 60).

The appeal not to receive the grace of God "in vain" is fortified by a quotation from Isaiah 49:8. A reading of the original context will reveal that these words are spoken by Jehovah the Father to Messiah the Son. In this Old Testament passage God speaks of a time to come which He describes as an "accepted time," a "day of salvation." That prophesied time has now arrived, says the apostle. The present age is the "day of salvation." So he and other true ministers seek to "give no offense," or, more literally, not to place a "stumbling block" before any person, lest the service of Christ be blamed.

"But in all things approving ourselves as the ministers of God, in much patience, in afflictions, in necessities, in distresses, In stripes, in imprisonments, in tumults, in labors, in watchings, in fastings" (6:4, 5). These verses tell of the *testings* of the true minister. All are faced with steadfast endurance—"in much patience." *Afflictions, necessities, distresses* refer to things more or less providential and outside the direct agency of men. *Stripes, imprisonments, tumults* are troubles brought on the servant of Christ by evil men. *Labors, watchings, fastings* are things which the

Gospel minister willingly takes on himself in order to further the work of Christ.

"By pureness, by knowledge, by longsuffering, by kindness, by the Holy Ghost, by love unfeigned, by the word of truth, by the power of God, by the armor of righteousness on the right hand and on the left" (6:6, 7). These are the *characteristics* of the true minister. The word translated *pureness* comes from a root meaning holy, not defiled with contaminating things. The *knowledge* in view here is of the Word of God. *Longsuffering* refers to patience and restraint in the face of very trying circumstances. *Kindness* is "the graciousness that puts others at ease and shrinks from giving pain" (Erdman). *By the Holy Ghost* makes clear the only power in which Paul wishes to witness. "By love unfeigned" means sincere love from the heart, not sham or pretense. The true minister will be approved "by the power of God" as shown in the result of his work. "By the armor of righteousness" he will be protected from all attacks of the enemy, knowing that he has the answer of a good conscience that his conduct is honest and upright. The "right hand" (v. 7) may refer to the sword held in the right hand for offense, the "left hand" to the shield for defense (cf. Eph. 6:16, 17).

"By honor and dishonor, by evil report and good report: as deceivers, and yet true; As unknown, and yet well known; as dying, and, behold, we live; as chastened, and not killed; As sorrowful, yet always rejoicing; as poor, yet making many rich; as having nothing, and yet possessing all things" (6:8-10). These verses display the *paradoxes* of the true minister. The apostle recites a considerable list of things, each of which is paired with something that seems to be its opposite, yet all are true of himself and each proves him a real Gospel minister.

He is both honored and dishonored. Both evil and good reports of him are circulated. He is called "deceiver" by some and yet he is true. He is unknown to the world in general, yet well known in Christian circles among people who *really* count. He is frequently near death, yet delivered and enabled to live on. He is chastened by God's hand, yet not slain. He is sorrowful (as in Rom. 9:2), yet always rejoicing (Phil. 4:4). He is poor in earthly goods, yet makes many "rich" with the true spiritual wealth. To the world he seems to have nothing, yet actually he possesses "all things" (cf. I Cor. 3:21-23).

M. The Call to Separation (6:11-7:1)

"O ye Corinthians, our mouth is open unto you, our heart is enlarged. Ye are not straitened in us, but ye are straitened in your own bowels. Now for a recompence in the same, (I speak as unto my children,) be ye also enlarged" (6:11-13). Before urging the Corinthian Christians to a place of separation, Paul makes a touching appeal for their love. He has "opened his mouth"; he has frankly and fully expressed his thoughts to them in this letter. There is room for them in his heart. If there is anything hindering and restricting the love which should exist between them it is not on his side but on theirs. They are "straitened" (the Greek word means *pressed for room*) in their own affections. To give him a fitting recompense for his own love to them as their spiritual father, they should make large room for him in their hearts.

"Be ye not unequally yoked together with unbelievers: for what fellowship hath righteousness with unrighteousness? and what communion hath light with darkness? And what concord hath Christ with Belial? or what part hath he that believeth with an infidel? And what agreement hath the temple of God with idols? for ye are the temple of the living God; as God hath said, I will dwell in them, and walk in them; and I will be their God, and they shall be my people" (6:14-16). One thing which evidently had been hindering their love for him was entangling alliances on their part with unbelievers. The figure of being "yoked together" may have been suggested by Deuteronomy 22:10: "Thou shalt not plow with an ox and an ass together." "The ox and the ass were chiefly used in husbandry; but, as they were of different size and strength, it was not only fitting that they should not be yoked to the same plow, but it might be cruel so to yoke them *(Pulpit Commentary,* Vol. III, p. 355).

This does not at all mean that there must be no contacts whatever between believers and unbelievers. "I wrote unto you in an epistle not to company with fornicators: Yet not altogether with the fornicators of this world, or with the covetous, or extortioners, or with idolaters; for then must ye needs go out of the world" (I Cor. 5:9, 10). "If any of them that believe not bid you to a feast, and ye be disposed to go; whatsoever is set before you, eat, asking no question for conscience sake" (I Cor. 10:27). "He warns against making such common cause with the pursuits and aims of unbelievers as might compromise

Christian character and destroy the integrity and distinctness of Christian life. His words are not to be applied only to marriages with unbelievers. They should include all those intimacies which arise out of business relations, secret orders, social activities, friendships and fellowships. Such intimacies, in themselves possibly innocent, may develop into unions which dwarf spiritual life, weaken loyalty to God, secularize the soul, and annul testimony to truth" (Erdman, page 66).

The apostle then argues against the unequal yoke in two different ways. First he asks five questions, all of which show the incongruity of a believer being yoked with an unbeliever. After this he gives a group of precious promises which show what God will do for the one who does take a position of separation unto Him.

In the five questions the striking contrasts should be carefully noticed. On one side there is *righteousness, light, Christ, faith, temple of God.* On the other there is *lawlessness, darkness, Belial, unbelief, idols.* (Belial is doubtless used here to refer to Satan; it is an Old Testament word meaning literally *worthlessness.*) These things are opposites and obviously cannot be brought together in any harmonious arrangement. "There can be no coalescing between the

things, straightness and crookedness, light and
darkness, between Christ and Belial. They cannot do it, and so surely as any attempt is made,
that which will suffer will be the high and true
and noble, not the low, the untrue, and the base"
(Morgan, *op. cit.,* p. 247).

Believers are God's spiritual temples. Quoting
from Leviticus 26:11, 12, Paul proves that God
does dwell with His people, working in and
through them ("I will dwell in them, and walk
in them"). So in view of these promises, Christians are urged to separate themselves from the
unbelieving world. "Wherefore come out from
among them, and be ye separate, saith the Lord,
and touch not the unclean thing; and I will receive you, and will be a Father unto you, and
ye shall be my sons and daughters, saith the Lord
Almighty" (6:17, 18).

As believers in Christ we are to be "in the
world" and yet not "of it." We are to have
nothing to do with the soiling, defiling things of
the world. If we take this stand, then God will
truly *be* a Father to us, and we will know by
actual experience what it is to be His sons and
daughters.

"Having therefore these promises, dearly beloved, let us cleanse ourselves from all filthiness

of the flesh and spirit, perfecting holiness in the fear of God" (7:1). Since we have such promises as those just quoted at the close of chapter 6, the apostle urges us that on the *negative* side, so to speak, we cleanse ourselves from all things that would defile either flesh or spirit. On the *positive* side we should seek to "perfect holiness" in our lives, doing all this "in the fear of God." It may be observed in passing that these words make it clear that there are some practices which defile the *body*, others which do not injure the body but contaminate the *soul*.

N. Joy of the Apostle Over the Corinthians' Conduct (7:2-16)

"Receive us; we have wronged no man, we have corrupted no man, we have defrauded no man. I speak not this to condemn you: for I have said before, that ye are in our hearts to die and live with you. Great is my boldness of speech toward you, great is my glorying of you: I am filled with comfort, I am exceeding joyful in all our tribulation" (7:2-4). Another moving appeal is made for the affection and love of the Corinthians. They are in Paul's heart. He is ready to live with them or to die with them. His pride and joy in them are great. The reason for this will be explained in the verses that immediately follow.

"For, when we were come into Macedonia, our flesh had no rest, but we were troubled on every side; without were fightings, within were fears. Nevertheless God, that comforteth those that are cast down, comforted us by the coming of Titus; And not by his coming only, but by the consolation wherewith he was comforted in you, when he told us your earnest desire, your mourning, your fervent mind toward me; so that I rejoiced the more. For though I made you sorry with a letter, I do not repent, though I did repent: for I perceive that the same epistle hath made you sorry, though it were but for a season" (7:5-8).

After a long digression which pictured the ideal Gospel ministry as exemplified in Paul, the apostle now returns to the matter of his own personal affairs. He reverts to this subject at the point he left off in 2:13. He describes his trials in Macedonia. He tells how he was comforted there by the coming of his fellow worker Titus and by the excellent report of the Corinthians which Titus brought. He is glad now that his previous letter made them sorry for a little while.

"Now I rejoice, not that ye were made sorry, but that ye sorrowed to repentance: for ye were made sorry after a godly manner, that ye might receive damage by us in nothing. For godly sorrow worketh repentance to salvation not to be repented of: but the sorrow of the world worketh death. For behold this selfsame thing, that ye sorrowed after a godly sort, what carefulness it wrought in you, yea, what clearing of yourselves, yea, what indignation, yea, what fear, yea, what vehement desire, yea, what zeal, yea, what revenge! In all things ye have approved yourselves to be clear in this matter. Wherefore, though I wrote unto you, I did it not for his cause that had done the wrong, nor for his cause that suffered wrong, but that our care for you in the sight of God might appear unto you" (7:9-12).

The reason Paul is glad they were sorry is because they then repented of their misdeeds and corrected the matters that were wrong. *Godly sorrow* produces the kind of repentance that seeks to rectify the offense. The *sorrow of the world* is simply shame at being found out. This type of sorrow works death and ruin. Their grief after receiving the apostle's original rebuke was of a godly nature. They were then *careful* to clear themselves of the charge of tolerating evil. They were *zealous* to exculpate themselves and to *avenge* the wrong which had been done. In everything they showed that they really wanted the will of God. The apostle explains that his chief purpose in the beginning was not so much to secure the punishment of the culprit, or to see that the person who had been wronged received his due, but rather to demonstrate his care and love for the whole church. If such a condition had been allowed to persist, the entire assembly would have been corrupted and defiled. "A little leaven leaveneth the whole lump" (I Cor. 5:6) .

"Therefore we were comforted in your comfort: yea, and exceedingly the more joyed we for the joy of Titus, because his spirit was refreshed by you all. For if I have boasted anything to him of you, I am not ashamed; but as we spake all things to you in truth, even so our boasting, which I made before Titus, is found a truth. And his inward affection is more abundant toward you, whilst he remembereth the obedience of you all, how with fear and trembling ye received him. I rejoice therefore that I have confidence in you in all things" (7:13-16) . With these words Paul reveals that he has been comforted by their good conduct. It also did his heart good to learn of the way in which Titus was blessed by his visit to the church at Corinth. Previously Paul had boasted to Titus that the

Corinthians were really sound at heart and truly wanted the will of God in their church. This boasting on his part is now vindicated. So the apostle expresses his full confidence in the Corinthians in everything.

Chapter Three

THE MINISTRY OF GIVING—TRUE CHRISTIAN LIBERALITY (chapters 8, 9)

A. The Good Example of the Macedonians (8:1-6)

Moreover, brethren, we do you to wit of the grace of God bestowed on the churches of Macedonia; How that in a great trial of affliction the abundance of their joy and their deep poverty abounded unto the riches of their liberality. For to their power, I bear record, yea, and beyond their power they were willing of themselves; Praying us with much intreaty that we would receive the gift, and take upon us the fellowship of the ministering to the saints. And this they did, not as we hoped, but first gave their own selves to the Lord, and unto us by the will of God. Insomuch that we desired Titus, that as he had begun, so he would also finish in you the same grace also" (8:1-6).

In the closing chapter of his first Corinthian epistle, Paul had given instructions regarding an offering for the poor saints at Jerusalem, which the church at Corinth was raising. In the present two chapters, he gives further information about this offering. The particular case he discusses has of course long ago receded into the hoary past. However his message contains basic principles of Christian giving and church financing. These are ever true and just as profitable for us today as when the epistle was written. "If modern Christians were familiar with these principles and were guided by these instructions of the apostle, there would never be need of special appeals, and the treasuries of all boards and agencies of benevolence would overflow" (Erdman, page 74).

At the time of the writing of II Corinthians, Paul was in Macedonia. He therefore begins this section by citing the example of the Macedonians as to their generosity with money. God bestowed His grace on the Macedonian Christians. At the same time they suffered great trials. Though their poverty was deep, nevertheless they had great joy. From such an experience was born their extreme liberality. They not only gave as much as they were able, but even beyond their actual ability. The striking thing about it was that they did this willingly, not after some sort of high-pressure tactics had been applied.

It seems that Paul himself did not suggest to the Macedonians that they have a part in the offering for the poor saints at Jerusalem. They themselves, having heard of the matter, insisted that they be permitted to take part in the project. Then they went far beyond anything the apostle had hoped in that they gave not only a liberal offering of money, but that first of all they gave "their own selves to the Lord." They wholeheartedly dedicated themselves to assist in the work of God which Paul was doing. This loving consecration of the Macedonians (possibly the Philippians) so challenged the apostle that he immediately determined to send Titus back to Corinth again, to encourage in them the same grace of giving.

B. The Supreme Example of Christ (8:7-9)

""Therefore, as ye abound in everything, in faith, and utterance, and knowledge, and in all diligence, and in your love to us, see that ye abound in this grace also. I speak not by commandment, but by occasion of the forwardness of others, and to prove the sincerity of your love. For ye know the grace of our Lord Jesus Christ, that, though he was rich, yet for your sakes he became poor, that ye through his poverty might be rich" (8:7-9).

Before urging the Corinthians to be generous in their giving, the apostle first compliments them on the other gifts which they manifested. They were abounding in faith, in speaking the Word of God, in knowledge of the truth of God, in diligence in Christian service, in love for the Lord's servants. To these the injunction is added: "See that ye abound in this grace also." Sad to say there are Christians today who possess these other gifts mentioned here, and yet do not manifest liberality in connection with their money.

However Paul does not wish to issue a command in this matter. Liberality to be a grace must be spontaneous. So he simply mentions to the Corinthians the example of others, and in that way gives them an opportunity to willingly demonstrate the sincerity of their love.

As in all other good things, the supreme example in the grace of giving is the Lord Jesus Christ Himself. He was once "rich" in Heaven's glory. Yet willingly, for the sake of lost sinful human beings, He became "poor." He humbled Himself to become a man, and then went on to the death of the cross. Through this "poverty" of His we now become truly "rich."

> Out of the ivory palaces,
> Into a world of woe,
> Only His great, eternal love
> Made my Saviour go.

C. Advice Concerning Giving (8:10-9:5)

"And herein I give my advice: for this is expedient for you, who have begun before, not only to do, but also to be forward a year ago. Now therefore perform the doing of it; that as there was a readiness to will, so there may be a performance also out of that which ye have. For if there be first a willing mind, it is accepted according to that a man hath, and not according to that he hath not. For I mean not that other men be eased, and ye be burdened: But by an equality that now at this time your abundance may be a supply for their want, that their abundance also may be a supply for your want: that there may be equality: As it is written, He that had gathered much had nothing over; and he that had gathered little had no lack" (8:10-15).

In such matters it has just been indicated by the apostle that he does not care to *command* Christians. So he now rather *advises*. The Corinthians had both planned and commenced to gather this collection the previous year. Paul urges them to put into effect now in actual performance the willingness they had originally shown. The readiness to give what we have is the thing that really counts. Oftentimes we would like to do good things which we are financially unable to accomplish. If this is true, the Lord knows and He gives us credit for the willingness. It is not therefore the *quantity* of the gift that matters but, so to speak, the *quality*.

Those who possess an abundance should help those who are in need. The Corinthian Christians should help the suffering Jerusalem believers. Some day "the shoe" may be "on the other foot." The Corinthians may be in need and the Jerusalem members may be able to as-

sist them. As an illustration Paul makes reference to the Old Testament record of the Israelites gathering the manna in the wilderness
(Exod. 16:18). The one who greedily gathered
more than he could use had "nothing over."
All that was left was found to be spoiled the next
day. This was done miraculously, of course. But
among Christians today is not the same principle
to apply? The one who has more than he can
use ought to help those who are needy. If he
tries to hoard everything for his own selfish pur-
poses, it will prove a curse rather than a blessing.
This does *not* mean that all Christians should
have exactly the same income. Nor does it mean
that diligent believers should patiently support
the lazy and shiftless (see II Thess. 3:10).

"But thanks be to God, which put the same
earnest care into the heart of Titus for you. For
indeed he accepted the exhortation; but being
more forward, of his own accord he went unto
you. And we have sent with him the brother,
whose praise is in the gospel throughout all the
churches; and not that only, but who was also
chosen of the churches to travel with us with this
grace, which is administered by us to the glory
of the same Lord, and declaration of your ready
mind: Avoiding this, that no man should blame

us in this abundance which is administered by
us; Providing for honest things, not only in the
sight of the Lord, but also in the sight of men.
And we have sent with them our brother, whom
we have oftentimes proved diligent in many
things, but now much more diligent, upon the
great confidence which I have in you. Whether
any do inquire of Titus, he is my partner and
fellow helper concerning you: or our brethren
be inquired of, they are the messengers of the
churches, and the glory of Christ. Wherefore
show ye to them, and before the churches, the
proof of your love, and of our boasting on your
behalf" (8:16-24).

In this paragraph, Paul speaks of a group of
three Christian men who have been appointed to
handle the offering for the needy saints at Jerusalem. He recommends from personal experience
each of the three. From this teaching comes another abiding principle, neglected sometimes now-
adays, sad to say. *Funds collected from Christians
should be handled faithfully and carefully.*

Of those selected to take charge of this gift,
Titus is first mentioned. Not only did he accept the exhortation of Paul to take part in this
matter, but he was already enthusiastic. He went
to them of his own accord, not just to fulfill an

assignment given him. It is striking to note that
it was his "earnest care" for the *Corinthians* that
prompted him in this endeavor, even more than
his concern for the Jerusalem poor.

Another Christian brother accompanied Titus
to help care for this offering for the impoverished
believers at Jerusalem. We do not know just
who he was, since he is not called by name, and
it is useless to conjecture in such a case. It is
expressly stated that he was well known in the
various churches and highly respected. He was
in fact chosen by the churches to travel with Paul
and assist in this particular project. The Greek
word translated *chosen* (v. 19) means "to stretch
the hand." This obviously signifies some kind
of voting. Money matters of this kind are to be
handled, on the one hand, "to the glory of the
same Lord." But, on the other hand, they are
also to be handled honestly "in the sight of men."

Paul is anxious that this collection be handled
in an honest and businesslike way, so that no
one may have cause to *blame* him. If the apostle
needed to be careful in such a matter, how much
more do we in dealing with funds for various
kinds of Christian work. "In the sight of the
Lord" who knows all things, our actions may be
absolutely honest. But we must also be careful

that such things be honorably handled "also in the sight of men." " 'In a field of melons,' says the Chinese proverb, 'do not stoop to tie your shoe'; for that will *look* as if you wanted to steal one of the melons" *(Pulpit Commentary,* Vol. 19, p. 197).

With the above-mentioned two men still another "brother" was sent. This man, also unknown to us, had often proved his diligence and ability in the business realm. All three are highly recommended by the apostle. The Corinthians are urged to show how right was Paul's boasting about their love and liberality.

"For as touching the ministering to the saints, it is superfluous for me to write to you: For I know the forwardness of your mind, for which I boast of you to them of Macedonia, that Achaia was ready a year ago; and your zeal hath provoked very many. Yet have I sent the brethren, lest our boasting of you should be in vain in this behalf; that, as I said, ye may be ready: Lest haply if they of Macedonia come with me, and find you unprepared, we (that we say not, ye) should be ashamed in this same confident boasting. Therefore I thought it necessary to exhort the brethren, that they would go before unto you, and make up beforehand your bounty, whereof

ye had notice before, that the same might be
ready, as a matter of bounty, and not as of covetousness" (9:1-5).

As to the actual collection, Paul says it is superfluous for him to write since he recalls how forward the Corinthians were a year ago in planning
this offering. He has frequently boasted of their
willingness. Now he does not want the friends
who accompany him to Corinth from Macedonia
to find that he was mistaken in this confidence.
In that case *he* would be embarrassed, and really
they would be even more ashamed. Therefore
he wishes this offering to be completed *before*
he comes to Corinth. Then he can give his time
entirely to spiritual matters and not have to try
to raise money in a way that might seem like
covetousness on his part. He wants the offering
to be a *bounty*. A *bounty* means "that which is
given liberally" (Webster's *New Collegiate Dictionary*, p. 100). The present teaching has been
called "the law of bounty."

D. The Happy Results of Liberality (9:6-15)

"But this I say, He which soweth sparingly
shall reap also sparingly; and he which soweth
bountifully shall reap also bountifully" (9:6).

The truth expressed in these words has been called "the law of quantity." The teaching is made clear by the use of a familiar figure as an illustration. If a farmer sowed just a few seeds of wheat in an acre he was planting, he would of necessity reap just a small return. Therefore if he expects to *reap* bountifully, he must *sow* bountifully. Money which is given to help others, or to assist in some useful form of Christian work, should never be looked upon as something thrown away, but rather as a spiritual *investment*. When we invest our substance in this way it will bring back to us a blessed return, both in this life and in that to come. The "law of quantity" asserts that the blessing will be in proportion to the liberality of the giver.

"Every man according as he purposeth in his heart, so let him give; not grudgingly, or of necessity: for God loveth a cheerful giver" (9:7). This is "the law of quality." It is not alone the *quantity* of a gift that counts. The two mites of the poor widow were adjudged by the Lord to be more than the large gifts of the rich (Luke 21:1-4). They gave just a comparatively small part of their total income, while she gave her all. However not even the *proportion* of the gift to the total income is the matter of final importance, but beyond this the *way* in which the gift is given is of utmost significance. It is to be done *willingly*, each deciding in his own heart, entirely between himself and the Lord, just what he will give. It is not to be done *grudgingly*—with regret—nor of *necessity* because of outside pressure, but *cheerfully*. The Greek word translated *cheerfully* is *hilaros* from which we get our English word hilarious. It really means *joyfully*. We are told that God loves a "joyous giver."

"And God is able to make all grace abound toward you; that ye, always having all sufficiency in all things, may abound to every good work: (As it is written, He hath dispersed abroad; he hath given to the poor: his righteousness remaineth forever. Now he that ministereth seed to the sower both minister bread for your food, and multiply your seed sown, and increase the fruits of your righteousness;) Being enriched in everything to all bountifulness, which causeth through us thanksgiving to God" (9:8-11).

The same God who loves a cheerful giver is able to "make all grace abound" toward such a one. It is a rule that God generally supplies such givers with all their own needs and a sufficiency to further assist others. To prove this, Paul quotes Psalm 112:9. This psalm pictures the good man who truly loves God. Such a man helps the poor, and his righteousness (that is, his good deeds) abides forever. To the bountiful sower, God is able to give more seed. Paul prays that He will do so in order that cheerful givers will reap ever increasing fruits. The cheerful giver will be "enriched in everything." Through his liberality others will offer "thanksgiving to God."

"For the administration of this service not only supplieth the want of the saints, but is abundant also by many thanksgivings unto God; Whiles by the experiment of this ministration they glorify God for your professed subjection unto the gospel of Christ, and for your liberal distribution unto them, and unto all men; And by their prayer for you, which long after you for the exceeding grace of God in you" (9:12-14). Their gift will accomplish several results. The need of the poor saints will be supplied, and they will give "many thanksgivings unto God," receiving it as from His hand. "By the proving of this ministration" the Jerusalem believers will glorify God for the Corinthians and pray for them. This will make for better understanding between these two groups in the early Church.

"Thanks be unto God for his unspeakable gift" (9:15). The section closes with a pointed reminder of the gift that God gave—the supreme gift of all. If He was willing to give so much, then we too should be liberal in our giving.

Chapter Four

THE MINISTRY OF THE APOSTLE—
VINDICATION OF PAUL'S AUTHORITY
(chapters 10-13)

A. Paul Asserts His Apostolic Authority (10:1-18)

T HUS FAR IN THE EPISTLE, Paul has been commending at least the greater part of the church members at Corinth. In the balance of the book he strongly defends his own apostleship. This was necessary because of false teachers who were belittling him in order to advance their own legalistic doctrine.

"Now I Paul myself beseech you by the meek-

ness and gentleness of Christ, who in presence
am base among you, but being absent am bold
toward you: But I beseech you, that I may not
be bold when I am present with that confidence,
wherewith I think to be bold against some, which
think of us as if we walked according to the flesh.
For though we walk in the flesh, we do not war
after the flesh: (For the weapons of our warfare
are not carnal, but mighty through God to the
pulling down of strongholds;) Casting down imaginations, and every high thing that exalteth itself against the knowledge of God, and bringing
into captivity every thought to the obedience of
Christ; And having in a readiness to revenge all
disobedience, when your obedience is fulfilled"
(10:1-6).

The apostle stoutly denies that he is living "according to the flesh." Although in this section
he must utter some sharp rebukes, he begins by
beseeching, reminding the readers of "the meek-
ness and gentleness" of Christ, which he seeks to
emulate. The statement in the close of verse 1
evidently reflects a slander which some opponent
had made against him. It was said that when
personally present with them he was very "base"
("lowly," A.S.V.), that is, humble and meek, but
that when he was far away writing to them he

became bold. This was no less than an accusation
that he was too cowardly to speak boldly when
present, as he had done by letter in First Corinthians. Paul answers by beseeching them that he
may not *have* to use such boldness when he comes
to them again. He is however quite ready to be
bold in person as well as in letter against any
who may really need such treatment. His reference is obviously to the false teacher or teachers
who had criticized him, saying that he walked
"according to the flesh" and was not a true servant of God.

The apostle makes a play on words by saying
that in a sense he *does* "walk in the flesh." He
admits that he is just a weak human being. But
the weapons he uses in the spiritual warfare he
fights for the Lord are not human weapons (such
as human reasoning, deceit, trickery). His weapons are spiritual ones from God and they are
powerful enough to pull down strongholds of
falsehood. By using such spiritual armaments he
is able to "cast down imaginations" (or better,
"reasonings"). The truth of God is able to overthrow all the proud systems of human philosophy.
The figure of battle is continued by the picture
of those once held in these human systems being
made captives of Christ, with their thoughts and

reasonings being brought into submission to Him.
Paul further affirms that he is quite ready when
the Corinthians have obeyed God's Word to bring
to justice any stubborn minority who remain dis-
obedient.

"Do ye look on things after the outward appearance? If any man trust to himself that he is
Christ's, let him of himself think this again, that,
as he is Christ's, even so are we Christ's. For
though I should boast somewhat more of our authority, which the Lord hath given us for edification, and not for your destruction, I should not
be ashamed. That I may not seem as if I would
terrify you by letters. For his letters, say they,
are weighty and powerful; but his bodily presence
is weak, and his speech contemptible. Let such a
one think this, that, such as we are in word by
letters when we are absent, such will we be also
in deed when we are present" (10:7-11).

Paul has apostolic power and is prepared to
use it if necessary. Certain men in Corinth have
a tendency to "look on things after the outward
appearance." They are quick to judge things
superficially by the way they appear at first glance.
It would seem in this section that the apostle has
one particular false teacher in view, who was making claims for himself and slandering Paul, so

that a minority were following this deceiver. The apostle asks that if any such person thinks he has some special relation to Christ, let him think again and reason out for himself that Paul too is truly a servant of the Lord. Even if Paul should boast more of his apostolic authority than he has already done, he would not be put to shame concerning his claims. This authority was given him, however, not to overthrow churches but to build them up. The false teacher seeks to *tear down* that which has been already accomplished; the true teacher seeks to *build up* the work. But Paul does not wish to speak further of his authority, because he does not want to seem "to terrify you by letters."

Because of verse 10, some modern readers have concluded that Paul was unimpressive in appearance and a poor public speaker. The very opposite could just as easily be claimed from verse 11. Verse 10 is actually a slander of his enemies (or possibly of the one leader already mentioned, since the literal Greek is not "say they," but "says he"). More likely the criticism was based on the fact that when present with them he had been meek and loving, while in his first epistle he had boldly condemned them for their divisions, immorality, disorderly conduct at the communion table. The apostle insists that if necessary he can be just as strong and plainspoken in person as he was in his letter.

"For we dare not make ourselves of the number, or compare ourselves with some that commend themselves: but they measuring themselves, by themselves, and comparing themselves among themselves, are not wise. But we will not boast of things without our measure, but according to the measure of the rule which God hath distributed to us, a measure to reach even unto you. For we stretch not ourselves beyond our measure, as though we reached not unto you: for we are come as far as to you also in preaching the gospel of Christ: Not boasting of things without our measure, that is, of other men's labors; but having hope, when your faith is increased, that we shall be enlarged by you according to our rule abundantly, to preach the gospel in the regions beyond you, and not to boast in another man's line of things made ready to our hand. But he that glorieth, let him glory in the Lord. For not he that commendeth himself is approved, but whom the Lord commendeth" (10:12-18).

The important thing is not to glory in other human beings, or to be commended by them, but to glory in the Lord and be commended by Him.

Paul has been insisting that the charge of his
opponents that he is cowardly is false. He is bold
enough to use his apostolic authority when and
if necessary. He confesses however that there is
one thing he is *not* bold enough to do—that is to
join the ranks of those who praise themselves.
He does not wish to add himself to their number
or even to compare himself with them. Such
people form their own little cliques, set up their
own standards of success, then praise one another
for having attained these standards. "These enemies of the apostle form a mutual admiration
society. . . . Such mutual admiration societies are
popular down to the present day. They may be
found even in religious circles" (Erdman). It
is always fairly easy to feel self-satisfied and com-
placent by comparing oneself with others. If we
look hard enough we can usually find somebody
that we feel we are equaling or even surpassing.

In reality these false teachers are not doing a
constructive work but are simply attempting to
lead away converts Paul has already won. The
apostle does not boast of things beyond the actual
ministry committed to him by God. The Lord
called him to do a particular work in a certain
field. This call included the evangelizing of
Corinth. (It should be remembered that Paul

never undertook to go to Europe until divinely
directed there by the vision of the man of Macedonia, as recorded in Acts 16:6-10.) So he was
not "stretching" himself "beyond his measure"
by preaching the Gospel to them. He was simply
doing the work committed to him by God. Therefore he does not boast of things which are really
"other men's labors," as these false teachers do
who are trying to corrupt that which others
founded. On the contrary he hopes that the
faith of the Corinthians will increase to the point
that they will support him in his desire to "preach
the gospel in the regions beyond," always however within the "rule" (or "province" A.S.V.;
or "limit," A.S.V. marg.) which God has set for
him. The false teachers have little interest in
doing such pioneer evangelization. They prefer
instead to take over the work of others, to "boast
in another man's line of things made ready to
[their] hand." Even in what God has truly
called him to do, the apostle Paul however does
not glory in himself or commend himself. He
prefers instead to be commended by the Lord.
He implies that God *has* commended him by
placing the seal of approval on his labors at Corinth and elsewhere.

B. Paul's Reason for Asserting His Authority (11:1-15)

"Would to God ye could bear with me a little
in my folly: and indeed bear with me. For I
am jealous over you with godly jealousy: for I
have espoused you to one husband, that I may
present you as a chaste virgin to Christ. But I
fear, lest by any means, as the serpent beguiled
Eve through his subtility, so your minds should
be corrupted from the simplicity that is in Christ.
For if he that cometh preacheth another Jesus,
whom we have not preached, or if ye receive
another spirit, which ye have not received, or another gospel, which ye have not accepted, ye might
well bear with him. For I suppose I was not a
whit behind the very chiefest apostles. But though
I be rude in speech, yet not in knowledge; but
we have been throughly made manifest among
you in all things" (11:1-6).

In the opening portion of this chapter, Paul
shows that the false teachers are seeking to under-
mine confidence in him so as to lead the people
astray from the simple Gospel message. To combat this insidious purpose he must assert his apostolic authority. He indicates that he is now going to have to indulge in "folly," so asks his read-

ers to "bear with me." He has just (ch. 10)
written of the foolishness of praising oneself, of
the folly of glorying in self. Now he of necessity must do something which may seem to be
the very thing he condemned. The original word
translated "folly" means literally "without reason," and refers to "a want of mental sanity and
sobriety, a reckless and inconsiderate habit of
mind" (Hort, quoted by Vine, *op. cit.*, p. 113).

The reason the apostle must indulge in such
"folly" is because he is *jealous* and he *fears*. His
jealousy however, it should be carefully observed,
is a *godly* jealousy. *Un*godly jealousy often causes
great trouble even in our churches today. Paul's
jealousy was not for *himself* but for *the Lord*. He
has "espoused" (or "engaged") the church in a
spiritual way to Christ. He has, in a sense, acted
as the "friend of the bridegroom" (cf. John 3:29).
He is therefore jealous that the church may remain loyal and devoted to Christ. (In his day
a betrothal or engagement was very serious and
binding; it meant much more than it sometimes
does with us at the present time.) "It must be
noted that Paul is referring here to the collective
church. To speak of a single soul as a bride
of Christ introduces conceptions which are un-
scriptural and misleading" (Erdman, page 100).

Not only is Paul jealous, but he is also *fearful*.
He is afraid that Satan, the old serpent, may be
able to beguile the Corinthians, even as he "beguiled Eve through his subtilty." His method
with her was to combine a modicum of truth
with a most damaging error in order to lead her
astray. The apostle fears lest Christians now be
likewise led astray from simple faith in the Lord
Jesus Christ.

Verse 4 is not easy of interpretation, but the
thought seems to be that if these false teachers
came preaching another Jesus altogether, and pre-
senting a different spirit and a different Gospel,
then the people might well be tolerant with
them, giving them a hearing. However there
really is no other Jesus. There is only one Gospel, only one Holy Spirit. These deceivers pretend to be serving that same Jesus and to be
preaching the same Gospel, yet they try to de-
molish the work of Paul and to corrupt his converts. It should be mentioned that some inter-
preters consider the verse in a little different
light, taking the statement, "ye might well bear
with him," to be irony or sarcasm.

Not only is Paul an apostle but he is "not a
whit behind the very chiefest apostles." His reference is probably to Peter and John, whom he

calls "pillars" (Gal. 2:9). His slanderers have contemptuously accused him of being "rude in speech." That his language was not polished oratory he freely admits. But regardless of elocution he had the true knowledge of God and His Word. This he gave to the people. His ministry among the Corinthians should have made this crystal clear.

"Have I committed an offense in abasing myself that ye might be exalted, because I have preached to you the gospel of God freely? I robbed other churches, taking wages of them, to do you service. And when I was present with you, and wanted, I was chargeable to no man: for that which was lacking to me the brethren which came from Macedonia supplied: and in all things I have kept myself from being burdensome unto you, and so will I keep myself. As the truth of Christ is in me, no man shall stop me of this boasting in the regions of Achaia. Wherefore? because I love you not? God knoweth" (11:7-11).

The apostle now alludes to the fact that while in Corinth he had not accepted any offerings from the people there (see I Cor. 9). He "abased himself"—he worked with his own hands to provide his own living. This was done in order that no criticism might hinder the Gospel work. It was so that *they* might "be exalted," might become children of God through the free preaching of the Gospel. In fact when the apostle was unable to secure his expenses entirely by his own labor, he received money from other churches such as that at Philippi. In a sense then he "robbed" others to do the Corinthians service. *His* boasting is that he makes the Gospel "without charge" (see I Cor. 9:18). He is determined that no one shall be given an occasion to stop him from "this boasting." Was it because he did not love the Corinthians that he refused to receive financial support from them? God knows that this was not at all the reason.

"But what I do, that I will do, that I may cut off occasion from them which desire occasion; that wherein they glory, they may be found even as we. For such are false apostles, deceitful workers, transforming themselves into the apostles of Christ. And no marvel; for Satan himself is transformed into an angel of light. Therefore it is no great thing if his ministers also be transformed as the ministers of righteousness; whose end shall be according to their works" (11:12-15).

Paul is extremely careful in all he does to "cut off occasion" from those who "desire occasion." There are always opponents observing him, eager-

ly looking for something they can criticize. He
wishes these critics would glory in the same thing
he does—in giving the Gospel freely to lost souls.
It seems implied that they are *not* like the apostle
in being willing to support themselves but rather
are covetous for money. They really are not true
apostles at all but "deceitful workers." They are
not authentic apostles of Christ as is Paul. They
have no call from the Lord as Paul had. Instead
they have "transformed themselves" into the appearance of apostles of Christ, while they subtly
seek to corrupt and thus to destroy His true
Gospel.

That men should do such wicked things ought
however to be no great surprise. Satan, who is
behind false teachers, transforms himself, pre-
tends to be "an angel of light." He did this with
Eve, deceiving her into thinking that God was
doing her and Adam a grave injustice by keeping
them from the tree of the knowledge of good
and evil (Gen. 3:4, 5). Satan also pretended that
he was trying to bring them into an experience
which would be good and helpful to them. Even
so his ministers—observe that Satan has *his* ministers, *his* servants—hypocritically pretend to be
"ministers of righteousness." The Judaizers who
try to corrupt the Gospel *claim* to be offering

the real truth and to be standing for righteousness. False teachers today put on the same sham. However their *works* show that they are not really concerned for righteousness. Their final end will be according to these evil works.

C. Paul's Sufferings for Christ a Further Proof of His Apostleship (11:16-33)

"I say again, Let no man think me a fool; if otherwise, yet as a fool receive me, that I may boast myself a little. That which I speak, I speak it not after the Lord, but as it were foolishly, in this confidence of boasting. Seeing that many glory after the flesh, I will glory also. For ye suffer fools gladly, seeing ye yourselves are wise. For ye suffer, if a man bring you into bondage, if a man devour you, if a man take of you, if a man exalt himself, if a man smite you on the face. I speak as concerning reproach, as though we had been weak" (11:16-21a).

Paul now demonstrates that his life itself gives testimony to his sincerity, as the lives of the false teachers do *not*. He once again explains that he is forced to resort to that which may appear to be senseless boasting. But even though they may think him a fool, let them listen while he does this "boasting." In doing this, he does not follow the example of Christ, who never boasted of Himself. This is not to say however that in the apostle's case such a procedure is not necessary. It is for reasons already explained.

Since many in Corinth "glory after the flesh," Paul will show that he has as much in this regard as any of them to glory in. Deeming themselves quite wise, they gladly tolerate "fools," therefore they can tolerate him in his "boasting." Verse 20 sheds considerable light on the bold methods of the false teachers. Unlike the apostle, they brought the people who followed them into "bondage" rather than into liberty. Instead of receiving no money, as was the case with him, they "devoured" the Corinthians. They exalted themselves and were overbearing to the people. If the "smite" of verse 20 be taken literally, they went far indeed. Because Paul had not behaved in such a domineering manner, some had reproached him with being "weak."

"Howbeit whereinsoever any is bold, (I speak foolishly,) I am bold also. Are they Hebrews? so am I. Are they Israelites? so am I. Are they the seed of Abraham? so am I. Are they ministers of Christ? (I speak as a fool) I am more; in labors more abundant, in stripes above meas-

ure, in prisons more frequent, in death oft"
(11:21b-23).

If these deceivers are bold to speak of their
own qualifications, Paul likewise can be bold. He
now proceeds to show his labors and sufferings
which prove him a true apostle. We ought to be
very glad he was led to "boast" in such a manner,
for not only does he prove his point, but many
little insights into his life are given of which we
would otherwise be ignorant.

He first emphasizes that he is a *Hebrew,* an
Israelite, a physical descendant of *Abraham.* It
must be remembered that the opponents who
most troubled Paul in his own day were Jews who
professed to be followers of Jesus Christ but corrupted the Gospel with legalism. Evidently such
people laid great stress on the fact that they were
true members of God's chosen nation. In this
respect Paul himself is everything which they
claim to be. *Hebrew* is a term referring to *race.*
The word was also used in New Testament times
for the orthodox Palestinian Jews in contrast to
the Grecianized Jews who living among the Gentiles had adopted many of their ways. *Israelite*
refers to *nation*—the chosen people of God. *Seed
of Abraham* has to do specifically with the covenant of blessing God made with Abraham and

his seed (Gen. 22:17, 18).

These false teachers claim to be *ministers,* or servants, of Christ. Paul says that he is "more." He does *not* state that he is a *greater* servant, a finer preacher, or a better teacher, but that he is *more active* in service for Christ than are his opponents. Notice in verse 23 the parenthetical expression, "I speak as a fool." In the original this is the same word used previously for *folly*—"without reason"—but with a prefix added to it making it even stronger. It would refer to one who is an absolute madman. The apostle is indicating again that he is acting like a regular maniac in seeming to praise himself in this way.

As proof that he is a more active servant of Christ, he mentions being "in labors more abundant." In I Corinthians 15:9, 10 Paul states that he is not only more active than any of the false teachers, but that he is more active than any of the other true apostles. The record in the Acts of the Apostles, while it does not relate all of Paul's experiences, sufficiently justifies this claim. He has endured too many beatings to try to number them. Some of these are mentioned in the two following verses. He has frequently been "in prisons." Only one such imprisonment is recorded in Acts before he wrote this epistle—that at Philippi (Acts 16). He has been "in deaths oft." "I protest by your rejoicing which I have in Christ Jesus our Lord, I die daily" (I Cor. 15:31). The meaning is that he was often at the very point of death. Here are actual examples from Acts: "And after that many days were fulfilled, the Jews took counsel to kill him" (Acts 9:23). "But the Jews stirred up the devout and honorable women, and the chief men of the city, and raised persecution against Paul and Barnabas, and expelled them out of their coasts" (Acts 13:50). "And when there was an assault made both of the Gentiles, and also of the Jews with their rulers, to use them despitefully, and to stone them, they were aware of it, and fled" (Acts 14:5, 6). "And there came thither certain Jews from Antioch and Iconium, who persuaded the people, and, having stoned Paul, drew him out of the city, supposing he had been dead" (Acts 14:19).

"Of the Jews five times received I forty stripes save one. Thrice was I beaten with rods, once was I stoned, thrice I suffered shipwreck, a night and a day I have been in the deep; In journeyings often, in perils of waters, in perils of robbers, in perils by mine own countrymen, in perils by the heathen, in perils in the city, in perils in the wilderness, in perils in the sea, in perils among false brethren; In weariness and painfulness, in watchings often, in hunger, and thirst, in fastings often, in cold and nakedness" (11:24-27).

In these calm but poignant words the apostle recounts specific instances of persecution, as well as some of the general sufferings, endured in his evangelistic tours.

"Of the Jews five times received I forty stripes save one"—none of these beatings is recorded in the Book of Acts. "The Jewish scourge consisted of two thongs made of calf's or ass's skin, passing through a hole in a handle. Thirteen blows were inflicted on the breast, thirteen on the right, and thirteen on the left shoulder. The law in Deuteronomy 25:3 permitted forty blows, but only thirty-nine were given, in order to avoid a possible miscount. During the punishment the chief judge read aloud Deut. 28:58, 59; Deut. 29:9. The possibility of death under the infliction was contemplated in the provision which exonerated the executioner unless he should exceed the legal number of blows" (Vincent, *op. cit.*, p. 350).

The three times Paul was "beaten with rods" is a reference to beatings given him by Gentiles. Only one such whipping is described in Acts—that at Philippi (Acts 16:22, 23). "Paul escaped

Roman scourging at Jerusalem on the ground of his Roman citizenship. It is not related that he and Silas urged this privilege at Philippi until after the scourging. It is evident from the narrative that they were not allowed a formal hearing before the magistrates; and, if they asserted their citizenship, it may have been that their voices were drowned by the mob" (Vincent, *ibid.*).

The *stoning* is described in Acts 14:19. None of the three *shipwrecks* of which Paul here writes are mentioned in the Acts. The disaster which occurred while Paul was being taken a prisoner to Rome (Acts 27) took place several years *after* the writing of II Corinthians. On one such occasion the apostle evidently was in the sea—the *deep* waters—for no less than twenty-four hours, probably clinging to a piece of wreckage. Whether the "deep" is a reference to some particular locality or to the ocean in general is hard to say. One ancient writer indicates that there was a place near Lystra called "the deep" where the bodies of criminals were thrown. The exact Greek word is used only in this verse.

Paul had been forced many times to make long journeys, frequently traveling by foot. During these trips he came into *peril* in the eight ways mentioned in verse 26: through *waters* (rivers

in Asia Minor are said to be subject to sudden
"flash floods") ; through *robbers;* through con-
spiracies sometimes by Jews, sometimes by Gentiles; through the agency of wicked men in the
cities; through the power of the destructive ele-
ments in the wilderness; through storms, piracies,
and other perils on the *sea;* through the devious
schemes of hypocritical enemies who pretended
to be Christians—"false brethren."

Still other afflictions were endured in Paul's
faithful fulfillment of his mission—weariness,
pain, sleeplessness, hunger, thirst, fasting (whether
voluntary or involuntary is not stated) , coldness,
lack of proper clothing. Has any *false* teacher
ever been willing to endure such trials?

"Besides those things that are without, that
which cometh upon me daily, the care of all the
churches. Who is weak, and I am not weak?
who is offended, and I burn not?" (11:28, 29) .
In addition to the items already listed, troubles
largely from the *outside,* so to speak, the apostle
has endured *inner* suffering, arising from his zealous concern for the work of the Lord. He has
a real love and deep interest in "all the churches."
When he learns of Christians who are *weak* in the
faith, his heart is touched with sympathy for
them. When he hears of any one being *offended,*

that is, having a *stumbling block* placed before him, he burns with indignation.

"If I must needs glory, I will glory of the things which concern mine infirmities. The God and Father of our Lord Jesus Christ, which is blessed forevermore, knoweth that I lie not. In Damascus the governor under Aretas the king kept the city of the Damascenes with a garrison, desirous to apprehend me: And through a window in a basket was I let down by the wall, and escaped his hands" (11:30-33). If Paul is forced to glory at all in himself, he will glory in those things which demonstrate his own personal weakness, such as the above. This he does that he may also show what Christ is able to do through a weak vessel if it is given unreservedly into His control. At this point he solemnly affirms that all he is saying is absolutely true, as some might perhaps be inclined to doubt his accuracy.

The apostle closes the chapter with an account of his escape from Damascus, which is related in Acts 9:24, 25. At first consideration, this particular event seems rather tame in comparison with other experiences previously itemized. The reader may therefore wonder just why it is described in detail. Two possible reasons may help to account for this: (1) To be let down from a

high wall in a basket, with soldiers all around
searching for the hidden person, may well be
more perilous than one might at first think. (2)
Paul may especially mention it since it was the
first suffering he had to face after his conversion.
No doubt a proud Jewish rabbi, who had come
into a city with great power and authority, would
consider it very humiliating to be forced to leave
in such a way.

D. Paul's Visions and Revelations a Still Further Proof of His Apostleship (12:1-10)

"It is not expedient for me doubtless to glory.
I will come to visions and revelations of the Lord.
I knew a man in Christ above fourteen years ago,
(whether in the body, I cannot tell; or whether
out of the body, I cannot tell: God knoweth;)
such a one caught up to the third heaven. And
I knew such a man, (whether in the body, or out
of the body, I cannot tell: God knoweth;) How
that he was caught up into paradise, and heard
unspeakable words, which it is not lawful for a
man to utter. Of such a one will I glory: yet of
myself I will not glory, but in mine infirmities.
For though I would desire to glory, I shall not
be a fool; for I will say the truth: but now I for-

bear, lest any man should think of me above that
which he seeth me to be, or that he heareth of
me" (12:1-6).

Paul finds it necessary to still continue his
"glorying" or "boasting." So he now proceeds to
cite wonderful experiences. *Visions* refer to
supernatural sights granted to men. *Revelations*
are the truths shown during such events. Paul
has had such ecstatic experiences too, and he
writes now of the supreme one. "Someone may
ask me, Did you ever have an experience like
that? Never. Do you think other people have
had it? Undoubtedly. I am certain that experiences like that have been granted under certain conditions to certain persons, and always
with a certain definite purpose. It is an interest-
ing experience. How often people have wanted
to tell me about their visions! I am always sus-
picious. I want to know what they had for sup-
per the night before! If people have visions of
this sort they are silent about them. Fourteen
years had passed, and Paul had never told about
them; and even now he could not tell. They were
inexplicable, unspeakable words, words not lawful for a man to utter. It was a high experience"
(Morgan, page 267).

Even after fourteen years, Paul says "a man"

rather than "I did it."   Not until the reader ar-
rives at verse 7 is the secret revealed that *he* is
the man.   The man Paul had a remarkable experience.   He was raptured—"caught up"—to the
third heaven, the place of God's abode.   While
there he heard unspeakable things which he could
not utter on earth.   Was he raptured *in the body,*
or was it simply an altogether spiritual event?
He affirms twice over that even he himself did
not know.   (Is this perhaps a hint as to our own
feeling should we be allowed to pass through death
to the Lord?)

If he was not allowed to tell of this experience,
why then was it granted at all?   Evidently for
his own personal comfort and strengthening.   He
could later have easily gloried in himself because
of such a marvelous opportunity, but he will not
do so.   If he glories in himself at all it will be
in his *weakness*—that God has used such a feeble
vessel as himself.   Paul had determined "not to
boast of anything personal, except of what may
be called my weaknesses" (Phillips) .   He affirms
that if he did glory, or boast, of such spiritual
attainments he would not be "senseless" for what
he states is the simple truth.   However he wisely
refrains from saying more about such matters,
lest there should be on the part of any one a

tendency to exalt him above what he outwardly appears to be—just a weak human being.

"And lest I should be exalted above measure through the abundance of the revelations, there was given to me a thorn in the flesh, the messenger of Satan to buffet me, lest I should be exalted above measure. For this thing I besought the Lord thrice, that it might depart from me. And he said unto me, My grace is sufficient for thee: for my strength is made perfect in weakness. Most gladly therefore will I rather glory in my infirmities, that the power of Christ may rest upon me. Therefore I take pleasure in infirmities, in reproaches, in necessities, in persecutions, in distresses for Christ's sake: for when I am weak, then am I strong" (12:7-10).

At the time when Paul was granted the wonderful spiritual experience just described, some fourteen years before the writing of the epistle, he also received something else quite different. This he speaks of as "a thorn [literally, *stake*] in the flesh." Many are the conjectures which have been made as to what this "thorn" actually was. It must have been of a physical nature because it is pictured in such a way as to suggest comparison with the stake on which a condemned man was sometimes impaled. Surely the Lord

must have led Paul not to specify the exact nature of this affliction so that all of us who have
"a thorn in the flesh," no matter what it may be,
may still apply the same teaching to ourselves
and find comfort in it. This *thorn in the flesh*
was used by Satan as a messenger with which to
buffet (or, *slap*) Paul, causing him mental as well
as physical anguish.

It is clear that at the time he first received this
"thorn" Paul did not view it as a good thing,
for three times he requested God to remove it.
Nevertheless God said "no" and left him with his
affliction. As the years passed the Lord showed
Paul *why* he allowed this infirmity to remain. It
was really a gift to keep him from becoming exalted with spiritual pride, and thus become a
"castaway." During the passage of those fourteen
long years, God spoke to the heart of Paul and
revealed to him that although He had said "no"
to the prayer, yet He would graciously give something better. He would not only grant Paul grace
to bear the "thorn," but grace to live victoriously
in spite of it. So now the apostle glories in the
various trials which demonstrate his weakness,
for they make him cling more closely to the Lord.
Thus he becomes truly strong.

It should be observed from this passage that

*God does not always grant physical healing in
response to believing prayer. Sometimes* He does
—but *not always.* Contrary to the thought of
many people, physical infirmity is not always altogether *bad.* Sometimes it is allowed for our
own *good.*

E. Paul's Unselfish Love for the Corinthians a Further Proof of His Apostleship (12:11--18)

"I am become a fool in glorying; ye have compelled me: for I ought to have been commended
of you: for in nothing am I behind the very
chiefest apostles, though I be nothing. Truly the
signs of an apostle were wrought among you in
all patience, in signs, and wonders, and mighty
deeds. For what is it wherein ye were inferior
to other churches, except it be that I myself was
not burdensome to you? forgive me this wrong"
(12:11-13). The apostle has now finished his
"glorying." He acknowledges again that he has
"become a fool" in so doing. But he has been
forced to write in this apparently foolish way because they "compelled" him to do so. When
critics slandered him, the Corinthians ought to
have answered. *They* should have said these
things about Paul, who is not at all behind even

the chiefest apostle although nothing in himself. These people had plainly seen in his ministry among them "the signs of an apostle." These signs consisted of patient, self-sacrificing ministry in giving out the Gospel, as well as in miracles such as all the apostles performed. The only way, says Paul again, in which he slighted the Corinthians was that he did not receive from them any financial support: "Forgive me this wrong." "There is exquisite dignity and pathos, mixed with the irony of this remark" *(Pulpit Commentary, op. cit.,* p. 292).

"Behold, the third time I am ready to come to you; and I will not be burdensome to you: for I seek not your's, but you: for the children ought not to lay up for the parents, but the parents for the children. And I will very gladly spend and be spent for you; though the more abundantly I love you, the less I be loved" (12:14, 15). Again, in contrast to the false teachers, Paul reminds the Corinthians of his tender love for them.

Some commentators are of the opinion that Paul made a second brief visit to Corinth not mentioned in the Acts. However there seems to be no real basis for such a conjecture. When he says here, "The third time I am ready to come to you," he does not by this necessarily

mean he had already paid two visits to the city.
He plainly says this is the third time he has been
ready to come.   Very likely 13:1 has the same
meaning that "this is the third time I have pur-
posed to come to you."   The *second* time he was
hindered from actually coming because of their
conduct (see 1:15, 23).

Because there is among them a wrong spirit
in the matter, he has previously received no financial support from them nor will he now do
so.   He does not intend to be burdensome to
them.   They are his spiritual children and he
desires to "lay up" for them rather than they for
him.   The more he demonstrates his unselfish
love for them in sacrificial service, the more they
ought to love him.   But even if they do not he
will still love and serve them just the same.

"But be it so, I did not burden you: nevertheless, being crafty, I caught you with guile.   Did
I make a gain of you by any of them whom I
sent unto you?   I desired Titus, and with him I
sent a brother.   Did Titus make a gain of you?
walked we not in the same spirit?   walked we not
in the same steps?" (12:16-18).   It is obvious
that certain of the critics were saying that even
though Paul took no money himself, he was just
using guile and was getting it through such emis-

saries as Titus. He calls on the people to witness the falsity of such a lie. Were not his friends whom he sent to them just as sacrificial as he was?

F. Paul Will Manifest His Apostolic Authority When He Comes Again (12:19-13:10)

"Again, think ye that we excuse ourselves unto you? we speak before God in Christ: but we do all things, dearly beloved, for your edifying. For I fear, lest, when I come, I shall not find you such as I would, and that I shall be found unto you such as ye would not: lest there be debates, envyings, wraths, strifes, backbitings, whisperings, swellings, tumults: And lest, when I come again, my God will humble me among you, and that I shall bewail many which have sinned already, and have not repented of the uncleanness and fornication and lasciviousness which they have committed" (12:19-21).

The apostle makes it plain that he is not writing in this manner simply to defend himself. He is not bringing his case to them as to judges. He rather speaks as before God, and with the purpose of helping and edifying them. He fears lest when he makes his promised visit he will not find them earnestly and humbly living the

Christian life, but the very opposite. If so he will have to manifest his apostolic authority in correction, and thus be found of them "such as ye would not." Therefore he warns against sins which were evidently special temptations to them. There are *sins of pride and self will:* debates, envyings, wraths, strifes ("factious rivalries"), backbitings, whisperings, swellings (or "puffings up"), tumults (or "commotions"). There are also *sins* which stem *from immoral practices of the flesh:* uncleanness (moral impurity) fornication, lasciviousness (the word in the original refers to "shameless conduct"). If Paul finds his converts guilty of such sins and unrepentant, it will humble him and cause him to mourn.

"This is the third time I am coming to you. In the mouth of two or three witnesses shall every word be established. I told you before, and foretell you, as if I were present, the second time; and being absent now I write to them which heretofore have sinned, and to all other, that, if I come again, I will not spare: Since ye seek a proof of Christ speaking in me, which to youward is not weak, but is mighty in you. For though he was crucified through weakness, yet he liveth by the power of God. For we also are weak in him, but we shall live with him by the power of God toward you. Examine yourselves, whether ye be in the faith; prove your own selves. Know ye not your own selves, how that Jesus Christ is in you, except ye be reprobates? But I trust that ye shall know that we are not reprobates" (13:1-6).

Again the apostle refers to his prospective visit to Corinth. When he comes he will if necessary exert apostolic authority. After a proper investigation has been made he will not spare those who have sinned. They have been questioning his apostleship, seeking "a proof of Christ speaking in" Paul. They should not need to do that. They should realize that Christ *has* spoken through him very powerfully to their own hearts. Verse 4 is a parenthesis, and verse 5 connects directly with verse 3. Instead of examining Paul they had better examine themselves — those who raise such criticisms—to see whether *they* are really true Christians. They seem to have forgotten that if they are sincere believers Christ indwells them, for they are manifesting little of His Spirit. They do have Christ unless they are *reprobates* — false professors. Paul hopes they will understand that *he* is not a reprobate. He is not falsely professing to be an apostle.

In the parenthesis of verse 4, the readers are

reminded that Christ was crucified through (literally, *in*) weakness. This does not mean that
He was too weak to help Himself. It rather teaches that He deliberately humiliated Himself to
become a human being, with the infirmities connected with human nature, one of which was that
He thereby made Himself subject to death. By
this "weakness" of God we received the atone-
ment. We do not however serve a dead Christ
but One who rose and now lives in resurrection
power. The apostle Paul in himself is just a
weak vessel, but he now lives with the Lord Jesus
in resurrection power, which he manifests to the
Corinthians.

"Now I pray to God that ye do no evil; not
that we should appear approved, but that ye
should do that which is honest, though we be as
reprobates. For we can do nothing against the
truth, but for the truth. For we are glad, when
we are weak, and ye are strong: and this also we
wish, even your perfection. Therefore I write
these things being absent, lest being present I
should use sharpness, according to the power
which the Lord hath given me to edification, and
not to destruction" (13:7-10).

The apostle prays that the Corinthians may live
godly lives, not merely to bring credit to his own

ministry but so that they may do what is right.
He wants this even though he is thereby deprived
of an opportunity to exert apostolic authority,
and some may still insist that he is a false apostle.
The affirmation that "we can do nothing against
the truth, but for the truth" does not mean that
certain pieces of opposition to the truth may not
succeed for a while, but rather that *in the end*
God's truth will triumph. Let us all therefore
work now for that truth, knowing assuredly that
we are on the "victory side." Paul will be glad
if he does not have any opportunity to display his
authority and so will seem "weak" because they
are walking with the Lord and are "strong." His
deep desire is for their "perfecting" (A.S.V.).
He wants to see in them real spiritual growth.

Again he explains that he has *written* these
words of rebuke so that he may not have to use
"sharpness" when he is *personally present* with
them. The authority granted him by the Lord
Jesus Christ was not given just for the purpose
of tearing down and destroying, but rather for
building up. (It should be noted however that
sometimes there must be a tearing down *before*
there can be a building up.)